Supporting Young Children to Cope, Build Resilience, and Heal from Trauma through Play

Now more than ever, there is a need for early childhood professionals to comprehensively integrate trauma-sensitive practices into their work with children and families. This essential resource offers instructional strategies teachers can use daily to support their students dealing with trauma in early learning environments. Readers will learn to create opportunities for children to use their natural language—play—to reduce their stress, to cope with adversity, to build resilience, and even to heal from trauma. Nicholson and Kurtz provide vignettes, case study examples, textboxes, photographs, and descriptions of adapted therapeutic strategies ready for implementation in the classroom. Practical and comprehensive, this book is ideal for both prospective and veteran early childhood educators seeking to understand trauma-informed practices when working with young children (birth–8) in a range of environments.

Julie Nicholson, PhD, is a Professor of Practice, Associate Editor of *Early Child Development and Care*, author, international speaker/trainer, and MBA candidate (2023) concentrating on finance and data analytics.

Julie Kurtz, MS, is an author and national speaker consulting and training on trauma and resilience. Julie is the founder and CEO of the Center for Optimal Brain Integration®.

Other Eye On Education Books
Available From Routledge
(www.routledge.com/k-12)

Trauma-Responsive Family Engagement in Early Childhood: Practices for Equity and Resilience
Julie Nicholson and Julie Kurtz

Trauma-Responsive Practices for Early Childhood Leaders: Creating and Sustaining Healing Engaged Organizations
Julie Nicholson, Jen Leland, Julie Kurtz, LaWanda Wesley, and Sarah Nadiv

Trauma-Informed Practices for Early Childhood Educators: Relationship-Based Approaches that Support Healing and Build Resilience in Young Children
Julie Nicholson, Linda Perez, and Julie Kurtz

Culturally Responsive Self-Care Practices for Early Childhood Educators
Julie Nicholson, Priya Shimpi Driscoll, Julie Kurtz, Doménica Márquez, and LaWanda Wesley

Empowering Young Children: How to Nourish Deep, Transformative Learning for Social Justice
Wendy L. Ostroff

Leveraging Socio-Emotional Assessment to Foster Children's Human Rights
Jacqueline P. Leighton

Global Citizenship Education for Young Children: Practice in the Preschool Classroom
Robin Elizabeth Hancock

Supporting Young Children to Cope, Build Resilience, and Heal from Trauma through Play

A Practical Guide for Early Childhood Educators

Julie Nicholson and Julie Kurtz
with Lafeshia Edwards, Jonathan Iris-Wilbanks,
Samantha Watson-Alvarado,
Maja Jevgjovikj, and Valentina Torres

Routledge
Taylor & Francis Group

NEW YORK AND LONDON

Designed cover image: Isaac's mural, photo by Ryan Kurada

First published 2023
by Routledge
605 Third Avenue, New York, NY 10158

and by Routledge
4 Park Square, Milton Park, Abingdon, Oxon, OX14 4RN

Routledge is an imprint of the Taylor & Francis Group, an informa business

ISBN: 9781032352619 (hbk)
ISBN: 9781032334325 (pbk)
ISBN: 9781003326113 (ebk)

DOI: 10.4324/9781003326113

Typeset in Palatino
by Newgen Publishing UK

Contents

Figures and Tables

Figures

Tables

Meet the Authors

Lafeshia Joy Edwards, MA, MHS, MHRS, DMHW, IFECTMHP, CEIM, is a mental health rehabilitation specialist who supports families with children from birth to age 5.

Jonathan Iris-Wilbanks, AMFT, CCLS, is a child life specialist and director of a child life graduate program at Northeastern University.

Maja Jevgjovikj, MA, lives in San Francisco and is currently working as an Early Head Start coordinator at an early care and education agency.

Julie Kurtz, MS, is an author and national speaker consulting and training on trauma and resilience. Julie is the founder and CEO of the Center for Optimal Brain Integration.

Julie Nicholson, PhD, is a Professor of Practice, Associate Editor of *Early Child Development and Care*, author, international speaker / trainer, and MBA candidate (2023) concentrating on finance and data analytics.

Valentina Torres, MA, LMFT, is a licensed marriage and family therapist and an early child mental Health specialist who consults and coaches in early childhood programs and with families.

Samantha Watson-Alvarado, MA, LMFT, is the Director of Mental Health Programs at the Early Childhood Mental Health Program in Richmond, California, and owns her own private practice.

Introduction

Ada, a 4-year-old girl, in our classroom recently witnessed her dad faint, her mother call 911, and the ambulance come and take her father to the hospital where he has been for the past week with an unknown diagnosis. Ada has not been able to use her words to communicate how she feels about her father's absence with me or the other preschool teachers. However, when she plays in the sand bin, she appears to be telling us a story about how she is feeling and the worries she has about her father.—

(Clairissa, preschool teacher)

We had a young child in our care center who had experienced significant abuse and was separated from his family at a very young age. All he ever wanted to do was play with the trains. He would lay on the ground and he was just mesmerized by them. We wondered if the trains were a symbol of a family: coming together, linking up, separating. The trains left and came back.

(Jenna Juarez Ornbaun, family support specialist)

When we observe the world of play with children, we can learn so much from them. When children play they share with the world what is going on inside of them. We may not know exactly what their play represents, but children learn quickly which

DOI: 10.4324/9781003326113-1

adults are curious, attuned, and caring about the story they are trying to tell us.

> The need for early childhood professionals to understand the neurobiology of trauma and how to integrate trauma-responsive practices into their work with children and families is more important than ever and will only increase over the next decade.

Children are Experiencing Stress and Trauma at Significant Levels

Half of the children in the United States have experienced one or more types of serious trauma (Sacks & Murphey, 2018). And this percentage is likely to be much higher in actuality. Initial data suggest that the global health pandemic has had a significant and negative impact on children's social-emotional well-being and led to an increase in childhood adverse experiences (Bryant, Oo, & Damian, 2020). Over 167,000 children lost a parent as a result of Covid (and these numbers continue to increase), putting them at increased risk of consequences such as traumatic grief, depression, negative educational outcomes, unintentional death, and suicide over their lifetimes (Kidman, Margolis, Smith-Greenaway, & Verdery, 2021; Treglia et al., 2021). Further, children—especially low-income and Black, Indigenous, and families of color—have endured a cascade of additional adversities as a result of the pandemic, including employment loss, food and housing insecurity, and learning loss from program/school closures, and lack of access to technology/broadband and child care among other factors.

Children of all ages are absorbing significant levels of stress from their families and communities at a critical and very vulnerable time in their developing brains and bodies. Given the current levels of adversity that children, families, and the early childhood workforce are facing across the United States, *the need for trauma-responsive practice has never been more urgent.*

And given the pervasive and long-lasting impact of our societal trauma, trauma-responsive practices "should not be perceived as just another thing that will come and go," but instead, need to be comprehensively integrated into all systems and services serving children and families (Thomas, Crosby, & Vanderhaar, 2019, p. 445). Dr. Bessel van der Kolk, a world-renowned trauma expert, shares in his book *The Body Keeps the Score* (2014) that we are at an important moment in history:

> We are on the verge of becoming a trauma-conscious society. Trauma is now our most urgent public health issue and we have the knowledge necessary to respond effectively. The choice is ours to act on what we know.
>
> (pp. 347, 356)

How Children Use Play to Cope, Build Resilience, and Heal

The research demonstrates that for trauma-impacted children play provides abundant benefits and buffers to their toxic and stressful experiences. Play is a safe place for young children to express their inner world of emotions by providing them with a voice or way to express non-verbally their big feelings. Trauma may leave children with an internal narrative, "I have no power or control," whereas play can provide them with agency and a felt sense of control over their make-believe world. Additionally, through their play, they learn to find solutions and to build coping skills and resilience. It is common that our youngest and most vulnerable children usually do not have the skill to talk about their concerns and feelings, especially when these are scary—they "play" them out. Through play, children tell stories about what they observe and learn about the world around them, their past experiences, the feelings associated with these experiences, and how they feel about themselves and the types of support they need and desire from others (Fromberg & Bergen, 2006). Play provides the necessary language to express their thoughts and feelings better than they are able to do verbally.

For children who experience trauma, play is a powerful tool that provides them with a context to transform the experiences that are overwhelming and frightening into manageable and predictable events that they have control over.

◆ A child who lost a parent to cancer might engage in repeated cycles of search and reunion play, in which a baby lion is searching for her mother in the forest but is unable to find her.

When children can act out their life experiences through play, they have a safe place to release their big feelings. Because they can play out a scary experience over and over, they have opportunities to change or reverse the outcome in their play.

◆ A child whose family lost their home in a fire might act out the role of firefighter who rescues others from burning buildings and brings them to safety.

The well-known child development theorist Erik Erikson explained how play is the most important context for children to make sense of what happens to them. It is in play that children create experiences that mirror the reality of their lives but then explore and imagine a range of different outcomes, including those they fear the most as well as circumstances they desire (Lieberman, Compton, Van Horn, & Ghosh Ippen, 2003). Gary Landreth (2002), a renowned play therapist, explains why play is the most accessible and developmentally appropriate format for children to communicate about their lived experiences and feelings:

Children express themselves more fully and more directly through self-initiated, spontaneous play than they do verbally because they are more comfortable with play. For children to "play out" their experiences and feelings is the most natural dynamic and self-healing process in which they can engage…children's feelings often are inaccessible at a verbal level. Developmentally they lack the cognitive, verbal facility to express what they feel, and emotionally they are not able to focus on the intensity of what they feel in a manner that can be expressed adequately in a verbal exchange…play is the concrete expression of the child and is the child's way of coping with their world.

(pp. 14–15)

Neurobiology of Stress and Trauma (Nicholson, Kurtz, Perez, Bryant & Giles, 2023)

Learning about how stress and trauma can impact the brain and behavior can help us better understand ourselves, the children, and the families. When we understand the neurobiology of stress and trauma, we can make better sense of behavior that is otherwise puzzling and confusing. Then our approach shifts from reactive to a trauma-responsive, healing-engaged interaction that includes empathy and compassionate curiosity.

The Hierarchical Nature of Children's Brain Development

The process of neural growth occurs sequentially from the "bottom up" (Perry, Pollard, Blakely, Baker, & Vigilante, 1995). The first areas of the brain to fully develop are the brainstem and midbrain (the midbrain is part of the brainstem), as they are responsible for the bodily functions necessary for life, which are called the autonomic functions (e.g., breathing, sleeping, blood pressure). The last regions of the brain to fully develop are the limbic system, involved in regulating emotions, and then the cortex, involved in language, abstract thought, reasoning, and problem solving. Because of the sequential nature of neural growth, if one "layer" of the brain's development is interrupted and/or impaired, the subsequent parts of the brain will also not develop properly. For example, if trauma damages the healthy development of a child's brainstem, the child's limbic system and cortex will not function optimally, which may show up as delays or impairments with language development or difficulty with social-emotional skills or cognitive processing (Figure 0.1).

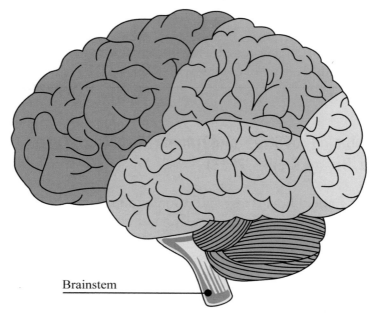

FIGURE 0.1
Brainstem.
Source: Courtney Vickery.

The Hindbrain (Survival Brain)

The first part of the human brain to develop in the womb and the first 2 years of life is the hindbrain. The function of the hindbrain is primarily survival. It makes us hungry so that we eat to sustain health. It triggers a tired feeling so that we sleep in order to restore our bodily functions and maintain health mentally and physically. The primitive part of the brain is also responsible for the *flight*, *fight*, and *freeze* automatic reactions humans have when they are faced with real or perceived danger. We all need this part of our brain to mobilize an emergency or survival reaction when in crisis. If a child puts their hand on a hot stove, their hindbrain gives them the fast-acting ability to mobilize reactions quickly and remove their hand so that they do not sustain burns. If an adult driver gets cut off on the freeway, it is their hindbrain that quickly reacts and makes them swerve swiftly away from a potentially fatal situation. This part of the brain is referred to as the "alarm center" or "smoke detector" (van der Kolk, 2014) and it continually scans the environment for signs of real or perceived danger. When it takes in data that trigger "danger" it dilates the pupils, increases blood pressure and body temperature, shuts down non-essential functioning such as thinking and reasoning, and sends signals to the part of the body needed to mobilize to safety through fighting, running away (flight), or becoming immobile as a last resort (freezing).

The Limbic Brain (Emotional and Relational Brain; Figure 0.2)

The limbic brain generates two big functions. The first is our feelings and the emotional intensity of feelings. The second function is attachments. Every mammal species is wired with a need to develop bonds of strong interpersonal relationships and attachments. Young babies are born with what is called "an experience-dependent limbic system," which means they need lots of repeated positive emotional, social, and cognitive interactions to support the development of a healthy emotional

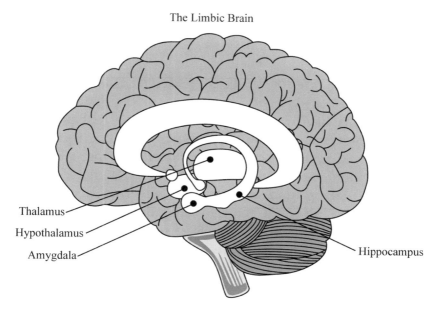

FIGURE 0.2
Limbic system.
Source: Courtney Vickery.

and regulatory limbic system (Conkbayir, 2017, p. 43). The limbic brain includes several different elements:

Amygdala (Alarm Center)

The amygdala controls our survival responses and allows us to react within fractions of a second to the presence of anything we perceive to be threatening or dangerous. It supports our ability to feel emotions and to perceive them in others around us and the physical sensations in our bodies that result when we are fearful or threatened (e.g., racing heart beat resulting from a sudden and very loud siren). It is the reason we are scared of things that are out of our control. The amygdala controls how we react to the events, experiences, and stimuli in our environments that are perceived as potentially threatening or dangerous. It is responsible for the development of fear and is often called the button in the brain that acts like an alarm alerting to danger.

Young children are less capable of regulating their emotions because the neural connections that communicate information from the cortex to the limbic system are not fully developed. Although the neo-cortex continues to develop until early adulthood, the amygdala is fully developed at birth, and for this reason, has a strong influence on young children's emotions and behavior.

The Pre-Frontal Cortex or Neo-Cortex (Executive Brain; Figure 0.3)

Only humans have a neo-cortex, allowing us to have more advanced processing capabilities. This part of the brain is responsible for making logical decisions, problem solving, sustained focal attention, self-regulatory capabilities, rational thought, perspective taking, and abstract thinking. The neo-cortex is considered the "air traffic control system or the chief executive officer" of the brain, but it dos not reach its full potential until the average age of 25. Just as a person does not become a CEO of a company overnight, it takes years of rich experiences and skill building to learn to manage a complex organization. Similarly, it takes our entire childhood, and into early adulthood, to build a strong neo-cortex. Positive experiences, nurturing caregivers, safe predictable environments, and factors that foster resilience

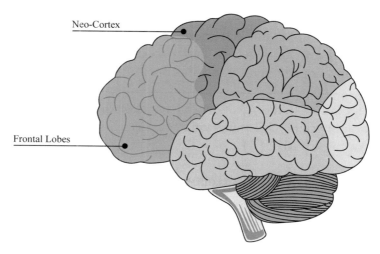

FIGURE 0.3
Neo-cortex.
Source: Courtney Vickery.

and buffer stress help build this part of the cortex brain to develop to its full potential. Here are some of the advanced functions of the pre-frontal cortex:

♦ **Self-regulation skills** involve the complex ability to regulate big emotions by finding practices that can buffer stress, promote calm, and regulate big emotions back to the optimal zone of arousal. Self-regulation also involves the ability to have self-awareness (what am I feeling and what is the size of my feeling?) and cultivate a pause to disrupt reactivity (through self-regulatory or co-regulatory strategies) to prevent harm to the self, others, or the things around them.

♦ **Executive function skills** include *working memory* (holding information in the short term), *behavior inhibition* (ability to pause before responding to a stimulus), and *cognitive and behavioral flexibility* (ability to change one's thinking and behavior in response to environmental stimuli) (Blair & Diamond, 2008). Executive functions work together to facilitate complex levels of self-regulation and problem-solving skills needed for children to pursue goals. For example, children use their executive functions to manage their strong emotions, motivations, and arousal levels to assist their ability to self-regulate and engage in learning and positive interactions.

Self-regulation skills and executive function skills work together to promote young children's emotional resilience (Center on the Developing Child, 2011).

Hindbrain / "Survival": Alarm Center of the Brain
- Fight, flight, freeze
- Breathing
- Heart rate
- Motor regulation
- Body temperature
- Blood pressure
- Reflex response
- Physical sensations associated with a traumatic event.

Limbic "Emotional/Relational" Brain: The Emotion Center of the Brain
- Attachment
- Emotional state/affect.

Pre-Frontal Cortex: "Executive" Brain
- Logic and reasoning
- Impulse control
- Self-regulation
- Problem solving
- Critical thinking
- Sustained focal attention.

Supporting Children to be in their Optimal Zone of Arousal

Arousal is a state of physiological and mental alertness. All children have an individual *zone of optimal regulation*, which is the arousal level where they are the most regulated and learn best (Figure 0.4). Too much or too little arousal can negatively

Hyperarousal

Children move out of the optimal state of regulation to a more hyperaroused state when they are triggered. Their alarm goes off and they are more sensitive and reactive to stimuli in their environment. They are unable to regulate their emotions and to have focal attention required for listening and learning.

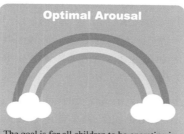

Optimal Arousal

The goal is for all children to be operating in the optimal arousal zone. This is the zone where children are regulated, calm and in an alert state. In this zone, they are able to think more clearly, listen and learn, have focal attention, follow instructions, express emotions and seek out appropriate solutions.

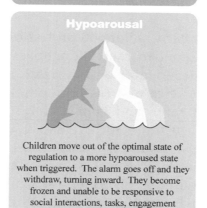

Hypoarousal

Children move out of the optimal state of regulation to a more hypoaroused state when triggered. The alarm goes off and they withdraw, turning inward. They become frozen and unable to be responsive to social interactions, tasks, engagement with others or the environment.

FIGURE 0.4
Zones of arousal.
Source: Courtney Vickery.

influence children's behavior and their ability to learn. There is a strong relationship between environmental stimuli and the arousal system. In considering how to support children to be in their zone of optimal arousal/regulation, teachers need to identify the type and number of stimuli children are exposed to:

Hyper-Arousal. If children are triggered, their arousal level shifts above their optimal threshold and they become hyper-aroused, which requires the need to release huge amounts of energy such as running away, throwing objects, throwing a tantrum, hurting others, yelling, or screaming (*fight/flight reaction*).

Optimal Regulation. The state of physiological and mental alertness that is optimal for children's behavior and ability to learn. The *zone of optimal arousal* is where children can function optimally and are able to access their cortex (executive brain) to focus, listen, reason, engage, and problem solve as they face difficult situations (*regulated response*).

Hypo-Arousal. If children are triggered, their arousal level shifts below their optimal threshold and they become hypo-aroused, which leads to behavior that is withdrawn. This may look like a child who is alone in the corner of the room and staring at the wall, low physical energy, low emotion, and low cognitive activity such as being despondent, shut down, hiding, unresponsive, or uninvolved (*freeze reaction*).

It is important for early childhood professionals to learn how young children respond to traumatic or toxic stress. It is a whole mind-and-body experience as they react neurobiologically (e.g., their bodies release stress hormones), physiologically (e.g., rapid heart rate), and behaviorally (e.g., inability to pay attention) when traumatic events stir up the children's feelings of helplessness and fear and trigger a complex set of chemical and neurological events known as a body's *stress response* (Massachusetts Advocates for Children, 2005). We know from research that if children grow up with persistent traumatic stress and fear, they can easily find themselves on an unhealthy neurological trajectory with significant damage to the development of their vulnerable brains (Siegel, 2012). Traumatic stress is most harmful in children's earliest years because it undermines typical development of the right hemisphere of the brain, which governs children's coping abilities and their emotional regulation (Schore, 2005, 2010).

Defining Trauma

Trauma affects children in every state, county, and city in America. Trauma impacts children and their families across all racial, ethnic, income, and education levels, family constellations, geographic locations, and community groups. Trauma has been described as our nation's single most important public health challenge (van der Kolk, 2014) that is too often silenced and unacknowledged for its significant prevalence and devastating impact. Trauma has been defined in a variety of ways by different scholars, clinicians, and agencies. Three important sources use the following definitions:

> Child trauma refers to a child's witnessing or experiencing an event that poses a real or perceived threat to the life or well-being of the child or someone close to the child (such as a parent or sibling). The event overwhelms the child's ability to cope and causes feelings of fear, helplessness, or horror, which may be expressed by disorganized or agitated behavior.
> (National Traumatic Stress Network, 2023)

> Individual trauma results from an event, series of events, or set of circumstances that is experienced by an individual as physically or emotionally harmful, and that has lasting adverse effects on the individual's functioning and mental, physical, social, emotional, or spiritual well-being.
> (Substance Abuse and Mental Health Services Administration (SAMHSA), 2014)

Trauma is the result of an overwhelming amount of stress that exceeds one's ability to cope or integrate the emotions involved with that experience. Trauma differs among individuals by their subjective experiences, not the objective facts.

(Statman-Weil, 2018)

Although trauma crosses all demographic groups affecting children in every community in the United States, young children of color and children living in poverty are inequitably represented in the child welfare system, foster care placements, and the national statistics on child maltreatment.

Early childhood trauma is a broad term that describes a range of reactions young children have in response to a stressful experience in which their ability to cope is seriously weakened (Massachusetts Advocates for Children, 2005). An event becomes traumatic for a young child when it overwhelms their nervous system's ability to cope with stress, leaving them feeling unsafe, vulnerable, and out of control. Traumatic experiences, whether real or perceived, lead children to feel significant levels of helplessness, powerlessness, and intense fear—experiences they perceive to be life threatening to themselves or others.

> Young children who experience trauma see the world as a dangerous place and their stress response systems are continually activated, communicating to them that they are not safe.

It is important to note that adults cannot determine whether a particular experience is traumatic for a child based on the intensity of a circumstance. This is because the experience of trauma is subjective and defined by its effect on a particular child's nervous system. While the intensity of a particular stressor is an important factor, this alone does not define trauma. As Peter Levine and Maggie Kline explain, *"trauma is not in the event itself; rather, trauma resides in the nervous system"* (Levine & Kline, 2007, p. 4, italics in original).

Traumatic experiences, whether real or perceived, are threatening and create intense feelings of helplessness, power-lessness, or terror and, in the absence of protective support from an adult caregiver, can have lasting and devastating effects on a child's physical, mental, and spiritual health (SAMHSA, 2014). Infants and toddlers are in the most vulnerable age group for trauma and experience the highest rates of child maltreatment (Stevens, 2013).

Prevalence of Childhood Trauma

Almost half the nation's children have experienced at least one or more types of serious childhood trauma (The Child and Adolescent Health Measurement Initiative, n.d.) This translates into an estimated 34,825,978 children nationwide. In 2016, an estimated 1,750 children died from abuse and neglect in the United States.

The Impact of Stress and Trauma on Young Children's Play

In most children's play we see a coherent storyline being acted out over time. With children who have experienced trauma we might not see this in their play. It's more of a stuck feeling or a theme being repeated over and over again. That to me would be a red flag that this child is communi-cating a story of what they have been through and that they need help from the adults around them.

(Jenna Juarez Ornbaun, family support specialist)

For many children, play is a regulating and joyous activity. Children who have experienced toxic stress and trauma might find the opposite is true. The impact of stress and trauma on children's play is significant and these children often need a lot of support to feel safe in the world so that their body relaxes enough to allow that present moment and joyous play to emerge.

Teachers of children who are overwhelmed by stress and trauma may see impacts of adversity on children's play:

♦ **Infants** exposed to trauma may be unresponsive to adult-initiated engagement cues to play and show very little interaction when introduced to toys and little interest in interacting with others in a playful manner.
♦ **Toddlers'** play is limited and often has a chaotic and purposeless quality.
♦ **Preschool children** often embed their fears and worries in play. Representing their own life experiences in imaginary play may prove too overwhelming and frightening.

Often, children affected by trauma have no joy, adventure, or imagination in their play. When they play, they might repeat the narrative of their trauma over and over, with negative emotion and aggression as key elements in play that feels stuck.

The themes in children's reenactment play can be disturbing (violence, death, injury, fear, abandonment), which can frighten other children and adults.

And many children living with high levels of stress and trauma are not able to play at all. As van der Kolk (2014) explains, "fear destroys curiosity and playfulness" and this can have a catastrophic impact on society. He continues, "we must raise children who can safely play and learn. There can be no growth without curiosity and no adaptability without being able to explore, through trial and error, who you are and what matters to you" (p. 350).

The purpose of our book is for early childhood educators to learn about the importance of play and practical trauma-responsive strategies that will support children's stress reduction, resilience building, and healing.

Balancing a Focus on Trauma with Coping, Resilience, and Healing

We believe it's essential to balance any discussion of trauma with an equal, if not more robust, naming of resilience, coping, healing, and strengths. No individual, family, community, cultural group, or organization wants to be defined by the bad things that happen to them (Ginwright, 2018). Focusing on our vulnerabilities and traumatic experiences can prevent individuals and groups from perceiving a felt sense of safety, agency, and control and, instead, can perpetuate cycles of trauma and oppression. In contrast, when stories of stress and trauma are honestly acknowledged but balanced with discussions of coping and resilience, we create the conditions to buffer stress, prevent negative impacts from trauma, and support healing.

> The American Psychological Association (APA) defines resilience as "the ability to adapt well to adversity, trauma, tragedy, threats, or even significant sources of stress" (APA, 2011). Instead of emphasizing the experience and impact of trauma, we need to spend more time fostering healing and strengthening the roots of well-being (Ginwright, 2018).

Resilience is evident in young children when their development progresses positively despite being confronted with negative experiences, including trauma. Research indicates that fostering young children's healthy development and their capacity for resilience is rooted in the following conditions:

◆ *Having consistent, supportive, and responsive relationships.* The most important factor in supporting young children to develop resilience in the face of stress and trauma is being part of a consistent relationship with a supportive caregiver who is responsive to the child's needs. Perry (2017) reinforces the power of relationships to buffer stress and heal, "Just as a traumatic experience can alter a life in an instant, so too can a therapeutic encounter. The more we can provide each other these moments of simple, human connection—even a brief nod or a moment of eye contact—the more we'll be able to heal those who have suffered traumatic experience" (pp. 308–309). One of the common themes that is well documented in research on resilience is:

"*Whenever there is evidence of resilience, you can always identify at least one very important relationship that was critical to the development of resilience.* Very often it's a parent, but it doesn't have to be a parent. It can be another member of the family, it could be a neighbor, a preschool teacher, a child care provider, a coach. It doesn't really matter who it is…But there has to be at least one person who provides a scaffold for a child to be able to cope themselves" (Shonkoff, 2022; emphasis added).

Resilience is also strengthened when children are supported to build healthy identities rooted in their family and community cultural ways of knowing and being and when they feel a sense of belonging.

◆ *Being in regulated environments with adults who buffer/ reduce significant sources of stress.* Children feel safe in the presence of adults who are regulated and calm and convey verbally and non-verbally that a child is safe and not in danger. Adults can help children back to the zone of optimal regulation and buffer a child's stress when they are an anchor of safety and support for a distressed child.

◆ *Perceiving a sense of agency and control.* As perception of a loss of control is one of the conditions of a traumatic experience, gaining a felt sense of agency and control is essential for coping and healing. In fact, Bessel van der Kolk (2014), world-renowned trauma expert, explains, "Resilience is the product of agency; knowing that what you do can make a difference" (p. 355).

◆ *Having opportunities to build core skills.* When children have support to build the core skills that are expected for their daily functioning in their families and communities, they are supported to have "the building blocks of learning, behavior and good health" (Shonkoff, 2022). For young children, core skills are best learned actively through play.

Adults who buffer the amount of stress a child experiences *and* guide them to develop self-regulation and executive function skills help children to learn to cope with the stressors and challenges they will undoubtedly face in life.

Play is the most effective context for young children to develop all of these foundations of resilience

Shonkoff (2022) predicts that in the near future we will have a robust evidence base showing that children's access to play is not only essential for their successful learning but also the foundation of their overall health and well-being. He explains,

> there is no question that somewhere down the road, maybe 20 years, we will all have an understanding that playful learning and the role of play in building resilience is as much about physical and mental health as it is about early learning and school achievement.

The Role of Play in Building Children's Resilience

> In the history of our species, we have used play as a way of building skills. Children use play as a way of mastering their environment. They learn to try things out. They test things and they test limits. Play is driven by curiosity and by an inborn drive to master the environment. If you think about what resilience is all about, it's mastering your environment. It's building the skills to be able to cope…to have some control with what is going on around you. None of that would develop as well as it does if you depended on just being "taught" on how to be resilient. *Your natural ability to play is one of the most important strategies that we have developmentally to build resilience in the face of adversity.*
>
> (Shonkoff, 2022; emphasis added)

Children need daily opportunities to use their natural language—play—to reduce their stress, to learn to cope with adversity, to build resilience, and even to heal from trauma.

Play is the most important job description for a child's growth and well-being. As Shonkoff reminds us, play supports children to experience mastery and to feel a sense of control and agency in their daily world. Play also supports children to learn to manage uncertainty and to have the capacity to "deal with anything that life sends their way."

But What Happens When the Hard Stuff Enters Play?

Many children are stressed and impacted by trauma and play is essential for coping and healing, yet few early childhood educators have learned what to do when the stories they tell in their play reflect their fears and suffering. So, what should early educators do when the "hard stuff" enters children's play?

The "Hard Stuff" Might Look Like...

- ◆ A 5-year-old girl who persistently locks up the father doll in the jail when she plays
- ◆ A 4-year-old boy who repeatedly burns down the house the dolls live in during play
- ◆ A 3-year-old who rocks himself back and forth on a mat in the corner of the classroom and won't engage in play throughout the day.

Because children use play to cope, reduce stress, build resilience, and process and heal from trauma, banning play deprives children of an essential vehicle for meeting their needs (Levin & Carlsson-Paige, 2005).

Unfortunately, most early childhood educators feel ill equipped or unprepared to deal with a child expressing their traumatic experiences in their everyday play. This has led to many early childhood programs where children's opportunities to play are being significantly reduced or eliminated altogether. *The answer is not to ban play in the classroom,* nor to dismiss or ignore children when they are hurting and need adults to acknowledge the frightening and sad things that happen in their lives. Instead, early educators need strategies that will help them effectively support children impacted by trauma in their classrooms to communicate, cope, build resilience, learn, and heal through play. Providing these strategies for educators is the main goal of this book.

With the prevalence of young children's exposure to trauma increasing significantly, there is a tremendous need for early childhood professionals to learn how they can create early learning environments that provide many opportunities for children to use their natural language—play—to reduce their stress, to learn to cope with adversity, to build resilience, and even to heal from trauma. These are the foundations that children impacted by trauma need in order to learn and develop to their potential.

Early Childhood Educators are Not Therapists

We recognize that early childhood educators are not therapists. We are careful throughout this book not to blur these professional lines of distinction between roles:

- ◆ **Early educators** work with young children ages 0–8 and are responsible for supporting children's learning and healthy development across multiple domains (e.g., social, emotional, cognitive, and physical development).
- ◆ **Child therapists** also work with young children; however, they are responsible for clinically assessing and treating children to cope better with mental health conditions that adversely impact daily functioning.
- ◆ **Mental health consultation** includes a variety of services within an early childhood setting:
  - • General consultation
  - • Child-specific consultation
  - • Program consultation

- Direct mental health services
- Training
- Advocacy and referral services.

◆ **Play therapists.** The Association for Play Therapy (APT) defines play therapy as an "interpersonal process wherein trained play therapists use the therapeutic powers of play to help clients prevent or resolve psychosocial difficulties and achieve optimal growth and development" (https://calplaytherapy.org/about-play-therapy/).

Every chapter includes examples of what positive and productive partnerships can look like between educators and mental health professionals.

Goals and Overview of the Book

Our goal in writing this book is to provide early childhood professionals working with preschool and early elementary-aged children with the knowledge and skills they need to understand trauma, its impact on young children's play, and a range of trauma-responsive practices they can use to create safe and predictable classroom and early learning environments that support children's health, healing, and well-being.

Audience for this book. The audience for this book includes anyone working directly with, or on behalf of, young children ages 3–8 and their families in addition to those responsible for the supervision of early childhood educators and/or providing instructional leadership for early childhood programs, including the following:

◆ Early childhood teachers, child care providers, instructional assistants, and support staff
◆ Site supervisors and directors leading early childhood agencies and programs
◆ New and experienced elementary school principals, assistant principals, and other public and private school administrators

- Educators enrolled in administrative credential programs preparing to be future principals
- Instructional coaches supporting early childhood program staff
- Other district administrators and support personnel with backgrounds outside of early childhood who will increasingly be asked to support and work with early childhood educators
- Professional development training and technical assistance staff and multisession in-service and professional development audiences
- Family engagement specialists
- Higher education faculty (e.g., early childhood teacher education programs, social work, general education, special education, psychology, administrative, and elementary credential courses)
- Researchers
- Mental health and inclusion specialists supporting children in early learning programs.

Book format. Throughout the book, we provide many vignettes, case study examples, textboxes, photographs from early learning programs, and descriptions of adapted therapeutic strategies early childhood educators can use right away in their work with children. As co-authors, we draw from our own professional work as well as from interviews we completed with early childhood professionals in diverse settings working across the United States. Every chapter concludes with key takeaways.

We are committed to making a positive difference in our field, especially for the children, families, and the early childhood workforce serving them in programs and communities that have historically faced, and continue to face, disproportionate levels of adversity and inequitable access to resources. *One small commitment we have made is to redirect the royalties from all of our books to programs serving Black and Indigenous children and children of color* doing powerful work to support culturally responsive and healing-centered practices based in love, healthy identity development, and healing. The royalties for this book will be directed to *Onkwe,* a group of Onkehonwe (Original Peoples' Mohawk name for people, meaning "original living being"), working in an outdoor learning space, to preserve their native language, seeds, ceremonies, and medicine. They share and teach traditional knowledge—including farming and gardening techniques—inherited from elders in order to return to the cultural ways they learned prior to colonization for children, youth, and families of all generations to come.

Jasmine Jimerson (Figure 0.5)

Teyútkwʌ niyukyats ukwehuhwéhne, ohkale Jasmine Jimerson niyukyats otslunike.
["She dances" is my Indigenous name, and Jasmine Jimerson is my English name.]
Yukwakwaʔho niyukwatalo·tʌ né oniʔ sʌ yukwatolahsko ne·n.
[We are of the wolf clan and also, we are of the great hunters.]

akwátsile̲.
[my family]

Onʌyotéʔa·ka   niwakyuhúntsyo·tʌ   talukowáne·ke   tsi yukwanushálu.
[Oneida is my nation, place of the duck (Oneida, Wisconsin) is the longhouse that we're tied to.]

My family moved to Mohawk territory to learn how to speak Kanien'kéha (Mohawk language) which we hoped would help us to revitalize our own language as Mohawk is the closest language to Oneida. When moving to Akwesasne it was important for me and my children to continue our responsibilities to the community and also learn about the knowledge that was held in the people, earth, plants, and water of this territory. We became involved with Onkwe, who became a family to us. We had the opportunity to learn about traditional relationships and knowledge sharing around food and plant medicine. Becoming and being a part of Onkwe were emotionally healing for our family and supported our physical health, which we needed to continue our traditional language and culture-based education.

FIGURE 0.5
Jasmine Jimerson, member of Onkwe.
Source: Jasmine Jimerson.

Chapter 1, *Learning to Observe and Value the Stories Children Tell Us through Play*, opens by describing how children share stories through their play about what happens to them, how they feel about it, and the type of support they need from adults to feel safe in early learning programs. Several examples are shared that highlight how early educators can respond in trauma-responsive ways when children communicate stories through play.

Chapter 2, *Building Consistent, Attuned, and Responsive Relationships with Young Children through Play*, provides examples of ways that early educators can tune in and mindfully focus on children and show genuine interest in understanding what their emotional states and/or behaviors are communicating through their play by shifting from a deficit stance (What is wrong with you?) to a trauma-responsive approach (What is your behavior communicating?). Several examples highlight how adults can support children impacted by trauma to develop a felt sense of safety as they play.

Chapter 3, *Arranging the Environment to Reduce Children's Stress and Support Healing through Play*, describes how early educators can arrange early learning environments to communicate safety and calm while reducing stressors and trauma reminders and supporting children to cope and build resilience. The chapter provides examples of different environment strategies and types of play that calm children's sensory response systems, including sensory play, play with structured materials, loose parts play, repetitive somatosensory play, big body play, dramatic play, expressive arts, and outdoor nature play.

Chapter 4, *Play-Based Instructional Strategies that Support Children to Cope, Build Resilience, and Heal from Toxic Stress and Trauma*, provides descriptions of instructional strategies and ways to organize the early learning environments for play-powered learning that supports young children to cope and reduce their stress. Authentic vignettes describe how early educators can embrace the stories (even scary ones) that children bring into their play and support them as they move through worries and learn to see themselves as having the ability to cope, build resilience, and feel safe.

Chapter 5, *Case Studies of the Power of Play to Support Children's Stress Reduction, Resilience, and Healing*, introduces six case studies that allow readers to go deeper into understanding how early childhood professionals are using play effectively with the range of strategies and approaches discussed throughout the book. Each case highlights a child in preschool or early elementary struggling with a traumatic stressor (e.g., neglect, implicit bias, loss of a deployed parent, impacts of the pandemic, impending move, etc.) and a range of trauma-responsive strategies adults can use to support them to cope and build resilience.

The end of the book includes important *resources*, including recommended books, apps, and websites for adults and children related to the content in the book.

References

American Psychological Association (2011). www.apa.org

Blair, C. & Diamond, A. (2008). Biological processes in prevention and intervention: The promotion of self-regulation as a means of preventing school failure. *Developmental Psychopathology*, *20*(3), 899–911.

Bryant, D. J., Oo, M., & Damian, A. J. (2020). The rise of adverse childhood experiences during the COVID-19 pandemic. *Psychological Trauma: Theory, Research, Practice, and Policy, 12*(S1), S193–S194. https://doi.org/10.1037/tra0000711

Center on the Developing Child (2011). Building the brain's "air traffic" control system: How early experiences shape the development of executive function. *Working Paper No. 11*. Cambridge, MA: Harvard University. www.developingchildharvard.edu

Conkbayir, M. (2017). *Early childhood and neuroscience: Theory, research and implications for practice.* New York, NY: Bloomsbury Academic.

Fromberg, D. P., & Bergen, D. eds. (2006). *Play from birth to twelve: Contexts, perspectives, and meanings* (2nd ed.). New York, NY: Routledge.

Ginwright, S. (2018). *The future of healing: Shifting from trauma-informed care to healing centered engagement.* Medium. Retrieved from https://medium.com/@ginwright/the-future-of-healing-shifting-from-trauma-informed-care-to-healing-centered-engagement-634f557ce69c

Kidman, R., Margolis, R., Smith-Greenaway, E. M., & Verdery, A. (2021). Estimates and projections of COVID-19 and parental death in the

U.S. *JAMA Pediatrics*, *175*(7), 745–746. DOI: 10.1001/jamapediatrics. 2021.0161

Landreth, G. (2002). *Play therapy: The art of relationship* (2nd ed.). New York, NY: Brunner-Routledge.

Levin, D. E., & Carlsson-Paige, N. (2005). *The war play dilemma: What every parent and teacher needs to know* (2nd ed.). New York, NY: Teachers College Press.

Levine, P., & Kline, M. (2007). *Trauma through a child's eyes: Awakening the ordinary miracle of healing. Infancy through adolescence.* Berkeley, CA: North Atlantic Books.

Lieberman, A., Compton, N., Van Horn, P., & Ghosh Ippen, C. (2003). *Losing a parent to death in the early years: Guidelines for the treatment of traumatic bereavement in infancy and early childhood.* Washington, DC: Zero to Three Press.

Massachusetts Advocates for Children (2005). *Helping traumatized children learn. Trauma and learning policy initiative.* Retrieved from www.massadvocates.org

National Traumatic Stress Network (2023). Retrieved from www.nctsn. org/what-is-child-trauma/about-child-trauma

Nicholson, J., Kurtz, J., Perez, L., Bryant, S., & Giles, D. (2023). *Trauma-informed practices for early childhood educators: Relationship-based approaches that support healing and build resilience in young children* (2nd ed.). New York, NY: Routledge.

Perry, B. (2017). *The boy who was raised as a dog and other stories from a child psychiatrist's notebook. What traumatized children can teach us about loss, love and healing.* New York, NY: Basic Books.

Perry, B., Pollard, R. A., Blakely, T. L., Baker, W. L., & Vigilante, D. (1995). Childhood trauma, the neurobiology of adaptation, and "use-dependent" development of the brain: How "states" become "traits." *Infant Mental Health Journal*, *16*(4), 271–291. Doi: 10.1002/ 1097-0355(199524)16:4<271::AID-IMHJ2280160404>3.0.CO;2-B

Sacks, V., & Murphey, D. (2018). The prevalence of adverse childhood experiences, nationally, by state, and by race/ethnicity. *Child Trends Research Brief*. Retrieved from www.childtrends. org/publications/ prevalence-adverse-childhood-experiences-nationally-state-race-ethnicity.

Schore, A. N. (2005). Attachment, affect regulation, and the developing right brain: Linking developmental neuroscience to pediatrics. *Pediatrics in Review*, *26*(6), 204–211.

Schore, A. N. (2010). Relational trauma and the developing right brain: The neurology of broken attachment bonds. In T. Baradon (Ed.), *Relational trauma in infancy: Psychoanalytic, attachment and neuropsychological contributions to parent–infant psychotherapy* (pp. 19–47). New York, NY: Norton.

Shonkoff, J. (February 22, 2022). *Building resilience through play*. Brain Architects Podcast. Center on the Developing Child, Harvard University. Retrieved from https://developingchild.harvard.edu/resources/podcast-resilience-play/

Siegel, D, J. (2012). *The developing mind: Toward a neurobiology of interpersonal experience*. New York, NY: Guilford Press.

Statman-Weil, K. (April 12, 2018). *Creating trauma sensitive classrooms*. Webinar presented by the National Association of the Education of Young Children.

Stevens, J. E. (2013). Nearly 35 million U.S. children have experienced one or more types of childhood trauma. *ACES Too High News* (blog). May 13, 2013. https://acestoohigh.com/2013/05/13/nearly-35-million-u-s-children-have-experienced-one-or-more-types-of-childhood-trauma/

Substance Abuse and Mental Health Services Administration (SAMHSA) (2014). *SAMHSA's concept of trauma and guidance for a trauma-informed approach*. Rockville, MD: SAMHSA. www.integration.samhsa.gov/clinical-practice/trauma

The Child and Adolescent Health Measurement Initiative (n.d.). *National survey of children's health*. Retrieved from www.childhealthdata.org/learn/NSCH

Thomas, M. S., Crosby, S., & Vanderhaar, J. (2019). Trauma-informed practices in schools across two decades: An interdisciplinary review of research. *Review of Research in Education*, *43*, 422–452.

Treglia, D., Cutuli, J. J., Arasteh, K., Bridgeland, J. M., Edson, G., Phillips, S., & Balakrishna, A. (2021). *Hidden pain: Children who lost a parent or caregiver to COVID-19 and what the nation can do to help them*. COVID Collaborative. www.covidcollaborative.us/initiatives/hidden-pain

Van der Kolk, B. A. (2014). *The body keeps the score: Brain, mind and body in the healing of trauma*. New York, NY: Penguin Books.

1

Learning to Observe and Value the Stories Children Tell Us through Play

Children Tell Us Stories through Their Play

Children use play to make sense of and organize their lived experiences. Gary Landreth (2002), renowned play therapist, reminds us that play is children's natural language and observant adults attuned to young children can learn to see how play reveals:

- ♦ What children have experienced
- ♦ Their reactions and feelings about these experiences
- ♦ What they wish, want, or need
- ♦ And their self-perceptions about who they are and how they belong in their families and communities.

When children bring their thoughts, feelings, and questions into play, they have the opportunity of a felt sense of being in control, even though the reality for young children is that they rarely do have control over the circumstances and schedules that dictate their daily lives. As Landreth (2002) explains, play is children's

DOI: 10.4324/9781003326113-2

method of finding a sense of balance and it is "the sense of feeling of control, rather than actual control, that is essential to children's emotional development and positive mental health" (p. 18).

> Children are able to use toys to say what they cannot say, do things they would feel uncomfortable doing, and express feelings they might be reprimanded for verbalizing. Play is the child's symbolic language of self-expression and can reveal: (a) what the child has experienced; (b) reactions to what was experienced; (c) feelings about what was experienced; (d) what the child wishes, wants, or needs; and (e) the child's perception of self.
>
> (Landreth, 2002, pp. 17–18)

Early childhood educators who understand that play is how children communicate can learn to observe and respond to the stories the children are telling us by promoting feelings of safety, security, attunement, and support. We outline throughout our book vignettes that give examples of providing trauma-responsive support to children during play without blurring the lines between an educator and a therapist.

Let's take a look at three examples showing how young children tell stories about what is happening to them and how they feel about it through play. We highlight three authentic scenarios in different early learning settings with young children. We describe children acting out their experiences through play and the trauma-responsive practices their teachers use to reassure and support them.

Example 1: Telling a Story through Play about the Global Pandemic

The first example highlights what early educators everywhere observed children doing in response to the global pandemic. Their lives, along with everyone in their families and communities, changed dramatically in a short period of time. Children brought what they were hearing, seeing, feeling, questioning, and worried about into their play. Kim Adams, owner of Barron Park Preschool in Palo Alto, California, describes how children used play to find a sense of control during a time when both children and adults were feeling such a profound loss of control:

> We had to close our center for about 2 months early on in the pandemic. When we came back, things looked different at school. Kids were having their temperature taken in the morning, grown-ups were wearing masks, there were so many changes, and it was a lot to process for the children when they returned. One of the first things we observed was the children using popsicle sticks to make thermometers and then using them to take each other's and the teachers' temperatures. They would call out the numbers "99," "98," "100". Play with the thermometers became a regular part of their daily play. They were acting out this very real experience through play. They were making sense of what was happening around them. It was the children's way of finding some power and some control over their lives at a very scary and uncertain time. *Children need control and power somehow. And play is often how they are expressing this need.*

Trauma-Responsive Practices in this Preschool

◆ *Through play children express feelings.* Kim recognizes that play is the canvas to act out the thoughts, feelings, and experiences a child is having. It is similar for adults when they talk to a trusted friend when something is causing them distress.

◆ *Attuned caregivers and safe environments.* When children feel safe with adults and in the environment, they can find a safe pathway to non-verbally express their feelings associated with a scary experience.

◆ *Agency, power, and control.* This preschool recognizes that when children feel a loss of control from a stressful or traumatic event, play can be the antidote by giving them a felt sense of agency, power, and control. Using their imagination to conquer a real problem provides the agency and control that can buffer their stress.

Example 2: Telling a Story through Play about Divorce

In the second example, we see a young child using play to organize and process his feelings about his parents' divorce.

Calvin is a young child (age 5) whose parents have recently divorced and now have shared custody. This new arrangement is painful and scary for Calvin. He has to transition from home to home and his regular routine and stable base have been disrupted. Both parents are preoccupied by their own recent stress. Calvin brings the story of his inner world of intense emotions, worry, and fear to the classroom. Teacher Lisa shares how Calvin found a way to communicate his life experiences through his play in the classroom:

Calvin was in the dramatic play area playing with two dolls, saying to himself, "This is mom and dad." He created two separate houses for the dolls to live in and then brought a little baby into his play. He started to fly the baby around like it was a bird. He then turned to Teacher Lisa who was sitting next to him and said, "The baby is a bird. The baby turns into a bird and flies away." Calvin continued flying the baby around the outside of the house, into the sky and then back into the house. The baby would play alone inside the house in a separate room from the rest of the family. Then Calvin would take the baby and have it fly away. Sometimes he would have the baby fly far from the house to a new location.

After observing Calvin's play, Teacher Lisa bent down to his eye level and asked Calvin, "Where is the baby going when it flies away?" Calvin replied, "The baby is flying away to get some superpowers." Continuing with open-ended questions with the goal of supporting

Calvin to perceive that she was listening to him as well as interested in learning more about what he was communicating through his play, Teacher Lisa then asked, "What do the superpowers do?" Calvin explained that he was visiting a magical princess who gives him some of her superpowers. "Wow," said Teacher Lisa.

She continued with another question, "Does this princess say anything or just give the baby superpowers?" Calvin did not answer and was quiet. Teacher Lisa took his lead and continued observing Calvin's play in silence. She noted in her mind that Calvin could tolerate her observing his play and asking questions, but not too many. After 5 minutes Calvin said, "It is a secret." Teacher Lisa nodded to acknowledge his comment, but she did not say anything. She wanted to be careful not to push Calvin past his window of tolerance as her primary goal was to increase his feelings of safety in sharing with her. Calvin then added, "Do you want to know the secret?" Teacher Lisa affirmed with a soft tone, "Yes," and Calvin said, "The magical princess has the power to bring mommies and daddies back together."

In this scenario, Calvin is processing his inner world of emotions as he plays with the dolls in the dramatic play area of his kindergarten classroom. He feels sad that his parents have separated, and he has a hope that a magical and mythical character can bring them back together. Through play, Calvin is telling a story about how he is feeling about and making sense of his parents' divorce. Play supports young children like Calvin to communicate a story about their internal world non-verbally, which is essential as many children have not developed the capacity to identify and communicate about their feelings or the experiences that cause them distress using words. In the presence of a safe adult, Calvin felt comfortable sharing his story.

Calvin proceeded to tell Teacher Lisa the secret, "Don't tell my mom and dad because I know it can't happen and I don't want them to be mad." Calvin knows this can't happen and that his parents will never come back together but his inner world is slowly processing the loss and sadness that come with big life events such as divorce.

How Play Supported Calvin's Ability to Cope, Build Resilience, and Heal

♦ During this play, Calvin had the opportunity to replace his feelings of grief and helplessness with opportunities for agency and control (e.g., superpowers, being able to control the narrative). He had a safe place to Name It To Tame It (Siegel & Payne Bryson, 2012).

♦ Also, the attunement by the teacher provided Calvin with the opportunity to communicate his feelings non-verbally through play.

Name It To Tame It

Dr. Daniel Siegel, an expert in interpersonal neurobiology, explains that when teachers invite children to share stories about their feelings and experiences they are helping them to calm their stress response systems. When someone shows compassion and takes time to listen to a child's story (told verbally, through drawings or play), this calms the emotional intensity within the right hemisphere of their brain. Expressing their inner world of intense emotions can reduce the energy charge in their bodies. After a child is able to share their story and emotions in a context where they feel heard and supported, they will become visibly more relaxed and appear calmer and more self-regulated. This process is often referred to as "Name It To Tame It" (Siegel & Payne Bryson, 2012).

Trauma-Responsive Practices Used to Support Calvin

♦ *Providing a safe and predictable environment.* When the classroom feels predictable and safe, then play becomes an opportunity to communicate the inner world of scary feelings a child is experiencing.

◆ *A trusted adult provides attuned relationships.* When adults build relationships with children, they become a safe person with the result that the child's body can relax enough to allow play to be the pathway for their story and feelings to be shared.

◆ *The teacher conveys empathy and curiosity for the child's feelings.* The teacher, being empathic, curious, and attuned to the child's play, helps the child develop a felt sense that "you see me, you care about how I feel, and you want to help me by listening to my story."

◆ *Prioritizing listening, not jumping to fix a child's big feelings.* Teachers who recognize that they don't have to jump to make a child feel better or help a child find a quick solution actually send a message to the child, "This big scary thing you are going through—I see it and I can be a safe base for you while you go through it."

◆ *Resources such as books for children can help them find new ways to cope.* The family asked Teacher Lisa about a resource to support Calvin after the divorce. Teacher Lisa recommended the book *Dinosaurs Divorce*, by Marc Brown. This story provided Calvin with an opportunity to see his lived experience mirrored back to him. Having mirrors (Bishop, 1990) is important as they acknowledge and validate children, which in turn reduces their feelings of "being different" from others. High-quality story books also provide children with models of how the characters cope with their stressors, reinforcing the message that "even though this is really hard, there are things you can do to manage it."

Example 3: Telling a Story through Play about a Community Fire

In our third example we are highlighting how children tell stories in their play when they experience community-based traumatic events such as a natural disaster.

Mario, age 6, and his family woke up in the middle of the night smelling smoke and hearing the sound of a local emergency warning siren. Their town in Paradise was burning down from fires ravaging through their Northern California community. Mario's parents quickly picked up Mario and Sandra, his younger sister, together with a few valuables, and they started driving. The streets were packed with residents fleeing the town and they could only drive a few miles an hour. As they drove, flames surrounded both sides of the freeway. Mario kept saying, "Are we going to die?" His dad, whose heart was racing with fear, managed to remain calm and reassure his son, "We will be fine," and he started to sing "We Don't Talk about Bruno" from the movie *Encanto* (Miranda, 2021), Mario's new favorite song. Though they made it safely to a temporary shelter set up for the evacuees, riding in the car while being surrounded by flames, needing to escape their home so quickly in the middle of the night, was a terrifying event for Mario and his family. Over the next few weeks, Mario began drawing pictures of fire while he was at preschool. Repeatedly, the same theme showed up: houses on fire, cars on fire, people on fire. He would set up cars in the dramatic play and reenact the scene of the flames surrounding the car and the family would escape driving through the flames.

Jessie, Mario's preschool teacher, understands that when children go through scary or life-threatening events, they are filled with big feelings. She is aware that big feelings create an energy charge in children's bodies that make them feel uncomfortable and agitated. This is in contrast to adults, who have the capability after a traumatic event to process their feelings verbally by talking to a friend or taking care of themselves to restore their stress by going for a run, being in nature, or surrounding themselves with the support of family and friends. Children have immature sensory systems and the most natural place for them to discharge their big feelings is through their play. Jessie's classroom environment provides children with many opportunities to communicate about their inner world—how they feel, how they are making sense of things, and what they are worried about—through their stories, pictures, and play. She observes

Mario and asks herself, "What is Mario communicating in these drawings?" Mario is communicating through play, *"I felt unsafe, I was scared, I am worried, and I am still terrified because of what just happened to me and my family."*

Jessie knew that she needed, first and foremost, to help Mario have a felt sense of safety in her classroom. She asked herself, "How can I send a message to Mario that I care, that I am listening to him, that I value his feelings?" Jessie used several trauma-responsive practices to reinforce messages of safety and attunement whenever she noticed Mario drawing pictures filled with scary fires.

First, Jessie just listened to Mario without using any words. She would sit in close proximity to Mario and observe. She understood that this was a way of giving him her attuned attention. By simply bearing witness to what Mario was communicating about his inner world as he drew his picture of being surrounded by flames, Jessie was reinforcing that he was not alone. *When Jessie provided attuned listening and her undivided attention, she observed it helped decrease Mario's stress. His shoulders relaxed down from his ears, his eyes moved from darting back and forth to being focused, and his fists stopped clenching as if he was bracing for danger.* She could see that the relational safety she was creating was supporting Mario to increase his felt sense of safety in the classroom and to express his feelings non-verbally.

Next, Jessie began to comment on what she was observing in Mario's pictures. "You are drawing a fire. The car is driving so close to the fire." Jessie used the strategy, *Say What You See.* This strategy provides additional attunement for the child. The teacher states what they are observing in the picture without a subjective emotion ("That must have been scary") or trying to fix the feeling ("Don't worry, they will be OK"). This listening tool is a powerful way to help the child know that you see and hear what they are experiencing in the moment as they reenact their scene of terror. *When a child is seen and heard it can calm their stress response system.* An adult can provide a "safe base." The adult can act as a calming, caring home base for the child to ground them when their inner state of emotions is overwhelming their stress response system. When a child is flooded with emotions, those feelings can hijack them to fight, flight, or freeze as a way of protecting them from the overwhelming feelings they are having. An adult providing co-regulatory and attuned support is like saying, "You are overwhelmed; borrow some of my calm state to calm your nervous system."

Jessie then began to comment and ask an open-ended question. "You are drawing a fire and a car is driving so close. Is there anyone in that car?" Jessie noticed that Mario's body was calm and more regulated after she had provided the attunement strategy *Say What You See.* She intuitively understood that Mario could tolerate adding an open-ended question. She asked him if anyone was in the car. This could activate his stress response since it is directly connected to his family in the car. Jessie asked the question when Mario felt safe with her, and his body was in the optimal zone of arousal. Jessie did not comment right away. His body moved slightly into tension with fists clenched and shoulders back up to his ears and his eyes began to dart as if in the middle of danger. She said, "Mario, you are with me in our classroom, and you are safe now. That was then, and now you are safe and your family is safe. I am here with you and will stay with you. You are safe here." He did not respond verbally but she could see his body relax slightly.

Careful observation of the child's non-verbal clues is important when working to create safety. Being trauma-responsive involves carefully observing how much a child can tolerate. A teacher can pay attention to the child's eyes, shoulders, hands, arms, mouth, and all the non-verbal clues children communicate through their bodies to tell us if they are ready to respond to open-ended questions. It is important to always think to ourselves, "Will my next action lead the child to regulation and safety, or will it lead them to dysregulation?" Asking an open-ended question should be done when we observe and believe they are ready (not observably in fight, flight, or freeze) and their executive cortex is more accessible (they are receptive and open to listen, reflect, think, or process in the present moment).

Mario is not ready for questions. When Teacher Jessie observed Mario's body (eyes darting back and forth, fists clenched, shoulders up to ears, facial expressions scrunched up, speed talking), she knew that the most attuned strategy was to sit near Mario and just listen and observe and/or sparingly comment on his play.

Mario signals he might be ready for an open-ended question. Once Teacher Jessie observed Mario begin to signal through his non-verbal behavior that he might be ready (calm face and body muscles, regular breathing pattern, relaxed facial expression, eyes looking at their play but back at the adult as if they are open to engage and talk, tone of voice, and speed of speech regular), she cautiously attempts the use of an open-ended question. When she asks the first question, she observes carefully: will this lead Mario to regulation or will it lead to signs of dysregulation? If his body tenses and/or he shows signs of moving out of the optimal zone of arousal, the teacher pulls back and continues co-regulatory and attuned relational support with minimal words. If he shows signs of being open, then she can proceed with another open-ended question. Reading the child's clues and taking their lead is important when helping a child to feel safe in the moment with us.

The goal for early childhood educators is to keep children within their level of tolerance. Creating safety through relational co-regulation will help children like Mario begin to tolerate more open-ended questions. When we follow the child's lead and listen to their clues (I feel safe with this strategy, or I don't feel safe with this strategy right now) then we teach them to listen to their body. We send a message, "Your feelings are OK, and this is a safe space, and we honor when your body says 'I need more' or 'I can no longer tolerate any more.'" We also help meet a child where they are at and for that child to feel loved just the way they feel in that moment. This act, repeated over and over, can help children cope and begin the journey of healing from their pain and the traumatic events they are experiencing.

Eventually, Jessie started to comment, ask an open-ended question, and seek a solution. "I see in your picture that the flames are all around the car and family while they drive. Is there someone or something that can help the family? Is there a helper who can put the fire out?" Mario smiled and said, "Yes." He added to his picture fire trucks and fire fighters holding hoses that are putting the fire out with water.

Jessie also introduced Mario to books that she chose because they promote resilience. In circle time, Teacher Jessie read the children's book, *Once I Was Very Very Scared* (Ghosh Ippen, 2017). She chose this book because it describes how each of the animals had been through something scary and how they all found ways to cope with their fears and big scary feelings. When reading the book, Mario would comment, "I was scared too. I was in the car and there was fire everywhere." Mario participated in the book reading with enthusiasm as he shared with other children that he too had been through something scary and how he sings his favorite song to help him feel safe when his heart is "exploding like a volcano." After reading the book several times during circle time, Mario added additional images to his drawings, such as his family singing in the car as they drove away from the fire. In time, his drawings started to change to show his family house with cars parked in front and the family inside his home playing together.

Jessie's communication with Mario's family. Jessie took time each day to check in with Mario's parents at drop off and pick up. She was very intentional in her choice to share with them the images in Mario's daily drawings. She also shared the specific ways she was supporting Mario to increase his feelings of safety at the preschool and to manage his big feelings. For example, she told Mario's parents about the books she selected to read with the children, as well as how she was supporting Mario to communicate his feelings through drawing and using a sensory and feeling check-in chart to point to what he might be experiencing in his body and how he might be feeling (Figure 1.1).

She shared how pleased she was to see that through this consistent support and reassurance Mario was building healthy ways of managing his feelings as he learned new resilience and

FIGURE 1.1
Sensory feeling check-in chart.
Source: Busy Bee Preschool.

coping skills. An example of Mario building a coping skill was evidenced by his adding a helper to his drawing who could put the fire out.

Jessie let Mario's parents know that acknowledging his fears is an important part of supporting Mario to work through them. She emphasized how essential it is that all three of them provide Mario with daily reassurance that his adult caregivers (parents, teacher, extended family, etc.) took care of him during the fire and will continue to take care of him every day and they will keep him safe. Jessie explained that research shows that consistent, caring, and attuned interactions are the most important intervention we can provide to children after a traumatic experience not only to help them work through big feelings and fears but also to prevent the development of long-term adverse outcomes.

Acknowledging Children's Fears Supports the Healing Process

There are many reasons adults do not feel comfortable talking with children about the scary events they see children experiencing or the terrifying images a child may show in their play. Here are some of the reasons teachers have shared:

♦ "I don't want to open up a can of worms."
♦ "It is not my business to get involved in the child's personal and family life."
♦ "I grew up in a family that only allowed happy emotions. So, when a child shows unhappy feelings, I am just compelled to jump in and make them feel better."
♦ "Only therapists can help children with their complex problems."
♦ "Honestly, I am scared I might say or do something wrong. So, I feel better not making any move rather than making a wrong move."

Adults have many valid fears and reasons and often think it is best not to talk about the experience when, in fact, acknowledging a child's fears is essential for their healing. A teacher is with the child for many hours in the day. A teacher has the power to be life enhancing and support a child in the present moment when they need a safe place to share how they feel and what they are experiencing. Play is often their best way. So, this becomes the canvas that we all can use to help a child cope, build resilience and heal.

How Play Supported Mario's Ability to Cope, Build Resilience, and Heal

♦ The scary images of the fire surrounding their car when they were trying to escape their neighborhood can stick to a child's memory like Velcro.™ A child can build skills to cope with those scary images or experiences by using play as a pathway for communicating the built-up energy charge that lives inside their body from that stress. Holding our feelings in is like holding in the steam from a kettle. Using play to communicate our feelings is like releasing the steam and built-up energy charge and helping us feel regulated and calm again.

Trauma-Responsive Practices Used to Support Mario

◆ *Listening to Mario without words.* Promoting safety and regulation in the present moment through our presence is the greatest gift we can give a child. Our presence conveys, "I am here with you now and I will do everything in my power to help your little body feel safe with me and in our classroom."

◆ *When Mario was ready, commenting on the pictures.* When Mario's cortex is available, he is ready to listen to comments about his picture and engage in back-and-forth conversation where the adult serves a question, and he has the capacity (optimal regulation) to listen and then respond back. Recognizing when children feel safe, their cortex is accessible and they are ready to engage is a trauma-responsive strategy. This is important because we want to choose pathways of engaging with children that take their lead in what they are ready for and how much they can tolerate.

◆ *Providing co-regulatory support.* The adult is the external calming and grounding source to the internal world of the child who may feel helpless and out of control emotionally or unsafe. Co-regulatory support is different for every child. Some need to be held, others need space but close proximity, some need to talk, and others need to convey how they feel through art or play. Learning to read the unique way a child needs support from an adult is being trauma-responsive.

Reflection/Discussion Questions

◆ Was there ever a time when you did not use words, remained quiet, yet were attuned with a child? What did it feel like to sit in silence but still convey "I am here, and I am listening" without actively jumping in to make them feel better?

Educators Need Support to Work Effectively with Trauma-Impacted Children

Early childhood educators have a tremendously important role in guiding children's healthy brain development. Young children's brain development is most rapid in the first 5 years (Conkbayir, 2017). Neural growth in the vulnerable and developing brain is strongly influenced by environmental conditions and a direct result of the various experiences a child has, whether developmentally supportive or stress-inducing and traumatic. Through consistent, attuned, and responsive relationships and environments where children have a felt sense of safety and belonging in their families and communities, children develop healthy synaptic connections that become a neurobiological foundation supporting their future academic learning and social-emotional health. Similarly, early experiences of chronic stress and trauma can impair typical synaptic growth, leading a young child's brain to develop differently, with potential adverse outcomes that can last a lifetime without proper intervention. For this reason, the early childhood years are absolutely critical. As Wolfe (2007) explains, early childhood educators not only support young children's learning, they are influencing children's biological wiring (cited in Rushton, 2011, p. 92).

Trauma-responsive practices cannot just be the responsibility of the teacher. The organizational systems in which they work can provide the much-needed buffers to their stress through intentional promotion of adult health and wellness, including opportunities for reflection. When teachers experience high levels of stress, they will not have the restored energy or internal resources to help trauma-impacted children who need regulated adults to help them feel safe and secure. Next, we will explore the types of support that teachers need to work effectively with children who have experienced toxic and traumatic stress.

Time for Teachers to Process and Reflect

Teachers who are working with trauma-impacted children need time and space to process their experiences, feelings, and observations. Without time to unpack their inner world of emotions, they have no other choice but to hold it all in. The long-term impact of holding everything inside could adversely impact their health physically, socially, mentally, and emotionally. Alternatively, for teachers who have a trusted relationship with another adult, they can rely on that relationship as a safe base. Talking and processing feelings allow a pathway to calm big emotions—Name It To Tame It works with adults too!—but also help support accessibility to the cortex where they can seek trauma-responsive and healthy solutions to their everyday dilemmas.

Don't Wait Until It's a Crisis

I would love for this book to change the way teachers and schools make decisions on when it's time to ask for help as the call is often made when things are out of control, the school is ready to silently push out the child, and the mental health consultant is a last resort. This puts so much pressure on the consultant to magically fix things very quickly in order to "save" the child and family from such injustice, train and teach the education staff on how to support the child in a way that is beneficial to the whole group of children, and all in a very short amount of time. This was one of the first pressures I had to navigate and breathe through when consulting with early learning programs. There was such a big pull to speed through the process versus slowing down and really seeing the child for who they were. I would meditate in my car before entering a site so that I could more easily stay in my center and with my breath. The pull was so strong.—

(Lafeshia Edwards, mental health specialist)

Many times the call for extra support is made too late and just before the program/school is ready to push the child out. That leaves so much pressure on the intervention and support service professionals to come in and feel pressure to fix the "issue" in a very short period of time. When teachers make that call for additional interventions when in crisis mode, they are in their survival brain. Then, the support provider has to try to fix things with a magic wand overnight, which obviously is rarely successful and not the way we heal trauma. It would be better for everyone if the call were made early on as a prevention strategy rather than when it is too late to intervene.

Though early childhood mental health consultation is intended to be a preventive strategy that supports teachers to improve their practice and intervene before children's behavior becomes dysregulated, unfortunately it is often used as a reactive strategy where programs try every other possible strategy before they attempt to access mental health consultants. This means that when the consultants arrive, early learning programs are often in crisis.

Following we describe a collaboration between an early childhood mental health consultant, Rose Messina, and three Head Start teachers—Wendi, Huan, and Pato—all working to support a 3½-year-old child, Luke. This story, told in Rose's voice, describes how she supported the teachers in cultivating a pause and slowing down to process and reflect and how that can be the very gift that can give teachers grace and restore their energy enough to provide the support that Luke needed to feel safe.

"I Just Wanted Someone To Tell Me It Would Be OK"

My name is Rose Messina, and I am a licensed therapist and have been working as a mental health consultant in early childhood for 15 years. Our Head Start program is in an urban area in a neighborhood with high cumulative risk factors (e.g., poverty, high crime rates). The program has access through Head Start federal funding to a mental health consultant to provide support to the classroom teachers and children one half-day per week.

Luke, a 3½-year-old boy, came to our Head Start program predominantly non-verbal, except for swearing or yelling and lots of intermittent hitting and destroying of things, from the profound neglect that he had endured. I think this was his way of communicating his pain and fear. Luke had been raised by extended family, Grandma and Grandpa, for the past year. Luke's story is a good reminder of the many ways that addiction can tear families apart. The family went through a lot of healing together and, by the end, the dad returned to this child's life. Yet, Luke's father was able to do a lot of healing as well. And once he could get in recovery and truly look at his own hurt, he could then be brought back into the family system.

When Luke would come to preschool, he did a lot of drawing, I think as a way to get out what was happening for him. Luke's drawings for the large part were very disturbing for most people who saw them. They were a combination of a robot that was bloody and had weapons and pokey things to protect it. And the first time I saw it, I honestly felt terrified and really did not know what to say and I asked him if I could hold the picture.

When I observed the teachers sitting with Luke drawing pictures, I noticed they tried to sit by him and draw. They would draw rainbows, flowers, and happy images and places where the scary robot that he drew could live. The teachers were understandably pulled to help him not feel pain. I mean, this makes sense, your first reaction is to want to take away the pain of a child! *But I think this little person really needed to know the adults could bear witness to what he had to tolerate.* And when we are able to talk about how painful it is to know that a child went through something so horrific, if we can believe it and tolerate it, we can join him and be with him and create a sense of grounding and safety. I felt the energy in the classroom when I visited, and it felt almost like a panic, a desperation, a deep sense of hopelessness and sadness that was in the air, and it was contagious. I knew they needed someone or something to help ground them so they could be there for this child.

Pause, Slow Down, Reflect, and Connect First

I called a team meeting with the teachers and myself. I thought it was important to cultivate a pause to slow down, take some time to think of what Luke may be feeling, and find a common language and some shared practices that we could commit to in order to create a secure base for Luke. The ultimate goal was to help Luke feel safe, to have others listen to his story, to learn to be present with the trauma he acts out and that lives in his body and that he projects to the world through the scary images in his drawings. To do this, he needed adults there for him without them shutting down or trying to make him rush to feel better. I just felt strongly we needed to cultivate a pause, take time to slow down, and reflect with one another. I believed we should take time first to tune inward into our own bodies, to gain self-awareness—to ask ourselves, how am I reacting to this child's story? How am I feeling when I see his drawings? How is bearing witness to his trauma impacting my physical and emotional health? I don't think any of us could help this child until we turned inward to name how we were all feeling. So, I guided the teachers in having this discussion. My goal was that after the teachers each named what they were feeling, we could then turn outward to provide trauma-responsive and individualized support to help Luke feel safe with us. None of us could get there yet, because we were so depleted and overwhelmed emotionally. We knew that we were not in the optimal zone of arousal (regulated and calm state) and that we were unable to access our cortex to plan, think, reason, or problem solve as it was shut down for all of us.

I really felt like the teachers were operating from a place I call burnout. I knew they needed some buffering for their own stress. I thought if we could slow down and support one another by talking about how we felt that might provide some protective support to one another, perhaps creating the feeling they are not alone and helping them to stop running on a treadmill and just slow down for a moment so we could create a space for them to feel and notice what was happening in their body. I was worried,

"Who is thinking about the teachers? Who is caring for them?" They needed grace and care and support and a safe space for them to process.

> Compassion fatigue results when adults become overwhelmed by the suffering and pain of those they are caring for… Individuals with high levels of empathy for others' pain or traumatic experiences are most at risk for compassion fatigue.
>
> (Nicholson, Driscoll, Kurtz, Wesley, & Benitez, 2019, p. 59)

I live by this quote adapted from Viktor Frankl: "In between a trigger and our reaction, there is a space in between (Pattakos & Dundon, 2017). In that space (or pause) is where we have the power to choose our response." We all were just reacting, and we needed the gift of a pause.

Each teacher had a different first reaction to witnessing Luke's drawings. Each reaction represents where we all can potentially go when our body is overwhelmed and we move out of the optimal zone of arousal because of too much stress. When our body can't take the stress any longer, the amygdala (alarm in our brain) can hijack us by triggering a fight, flight, or freeze (survival/hindbrain) reaction to protect us from real or perceived danger.

Teacher Wendi: Freeze reaction. "I just wanted someone to tell me it would be OK. Seeing his photos, hearing the story of what he went through, just nearly broke my heart. It reminded me of my own childhood, living with an alcoholic father who never really saw me and was not engaged. He was there but never really present. I just want to save Luke because no one ever saved me. When I am around Luke and I see his drawing, my heart starts to race, I feel a strong urge to run out of the classroom. I know I can't, so I just shut down. I feel like a frozen iceberg and honestly,

I cannot even move. So, in my freeze, I just ignore Luke. He needs me but I just look at him with a blank stare and ignore him. I feel so horrible. I can't seem to help myself and I hate myself for it."

Teacher Huan: Fight reaction. "I am so angry. Who would do this to a child? That father, I don't care who says he has healed. He will never be allowed to step foot in this classroom. People do not change. He won't change. I just can't contain how angry I feel that someone would do this to an innocent child. Sometimes I go home at night, and I feel on edge. So very much on edge that I take it out on my family by snapping at everything they do. I can't shake the anger and it is spilling over into my family life. In fact, all I can think about at home is how I want to look for another job. I mean I love the kids, I love my job, but I can't stop thinking and talking with my family about leaving."

Teacher Pato: Flight reaction. "I wake up each morning and feel like, 'Do I have to go to work today?' I wake up really not wanting to go in to be with the children. I have never felt that in my life! My home life was wonderful, but work was spilling into my home life and living with me there and I could not leave it at work. But I dredge myself up and drag myself in each day. But recently, it got worse. I started having really bad physical symptoms like stomach aches and headaches. For the first time, I had a migraine and had to call in sick. I started calling in sick at least once a week, but I wanted to every day. Everything was taking a toll. The stress was taking a toll. I just felt out of control. All I ever wanted since I was a little girl was to help children. I now felt like a failure in my job."

And so, we talked and talked as a team together. We talked about our families, we talked about how we felt, we talked about this child. We cried, we laughed. There was something powerful in being able to release how we felt in the presence of others who cared. I noticed that after a few meetings, the teachers were beginning to feel calmer, and I could see signs that they had restored energy. They began to signal that they were ready to talk about solutions. They had spoken about Luke, and now agreed they wanted to find strategies that would help him.

Together we learned to have an openness to bear witness to Luke's story and not try to soften the story for our own comfort. We recognized that Luke may not have words but could express himself through his art. We understood the importance of Luke naming his feelings and that the healing process involves not just naming them but feeling them. If we could support him in this process to express himself and to feel safe, only then could we begin the journey of helping him build coping skills. Our mantra became, "If he can sit in the discomfort of the trauma that lives inside his body, we can sit right by him and tolerate it too." *We wanted to create a strong and secure base for Luke.*

That pause seemed to be life changing for all of us. I feel like connecting with one another allowed us to have a restored energy to be able to think and problem solve more clearly."

We Can't Help Others Until We Have Support Ourselves

The reflective process is remembering, reviewing and thinking out loud about a specific child, the people who surround that child and what happens (or doesn't) between them. Reflection enhances vision, clarifying what is seen and even what is see-able.

(Shamoon-Shanok, 2006)

Rose could see the impact stress was having on the teachers. She was supporting them in slowing them down so they could be less reactive and more reflective. By prioritizing the following practices, she was creating a safe place for the teachers to process their own feelings of overwhelm:

◆ Time to slow down and pause
◆ Support in noticing the sensations and feelings inside their bodies

- Time to talk and reflect
- Time and space to tell their stories: how is this child impacting me personally or professionally?
- Creating relational support for one another to buffer the toxic stress they were experiencing
- Regulating the teachers' survival/hindbrain (fight, flight, freeze reactions and limbic brain with high emotional intensity) so they can access and open their cortex region (thinking, self-regulation, problem solving) and map out a trauma-responsive and resilience-building individualized plan for Luke.

Creating a Trauma-Responsive Individualized Support Plan for Luke

The teachers reinforced relational attunement for Luke in several ways:

- *Being present and listening to Luke* so that he felt deep within "they see me, they care about me, and someone can tolerate seeing that scary thing that kept happening to me when I was left alone in a room, and no one was there for me."
- *Describing what Luke was drawing.* For example, they would make comments such as, "That monster has pokies on it." "That monster looks like it has claws." This was to help him name what was happening in the drawing and/or his feelings associated with the picture. When the teachers narrated what they saw (of course, only when Luke could tolerate it), they were supporting Luke to learn how to express his inner world that felt scary and unsafe.
- *Adding feeling words to these descriptions and open-ended questions when Luke could maintain his "window of optimal arousal."* For example, saying, "That looks like it might be scary" or "I wonder if anyone is scared of this monster?" The teachers were aiming to insert language about what the monster felt like for Luke. Adding these comments

and questions can be challenging (because it's important to scaffold a bridge to a new possibility but to work to keep Luke inside the window of optimal arousal). It takes time for teachers to observe and notice if a child gets dysregulated by the comments and/or questions. If they do, it is important to step back and be less intrusive by attuning through observation only, while reducing the number of direct prompts/inquiry questions.

◆ *Working in partnership with Luke's family.* Rose explained, "We engaged Luke's grandparents. We did not want to begin a strategy without them being on board. We wanted to make sure they provided input, and we were responsive to their wisdom and expertise. Because of the relational trust that was developed, the grandparents were quickly on board with the support plan for Luke."

◆ *Drawing pictures next to Luke.* The teachers did this for several reasons. Luke did not know how to play with others. So, first we had to sit near him (he could tolerate one teacher, not touching him, and a few feet away). The teacher wanted to draw next to him as an act of playing with him and to communicate a feeling of inclusion and belonging as this is a way to buffer a child's stress by decreasing their feelings of isolation. At first the pictures the teachers drew were neutral—e.g., houses, dogs, rainbows—just to get him to tolerate parallel play. After Luke was willing to let one of the teachers draw with him, they added a new task into this parallel-play activity—drawing friendly monsters. Specifically, a friendly-looking monster that could invite Luke to play, a monster that was nice, wants a hug, wants to help. The goal was to help him find a way to build a relationship and connection with another monster which could be the foundation that allowed Luke to eventually build trust, feel safe, use words, and build a connection with other people like his teachers and the children in the classroom.

◆ *Repetition and patience.* Healing requires repetition of safety messages in many different ways and in regular doses.

Supporting the teachers to do this drawing with Luke was one way that Rose was partnering with them to learn how to support Luke and attune to his needs without centering their own need for comfort. They all knew the drawings they did next to him were not intended to send a message to Luke, "Be happy." Instead, they provided attunement: "You are drawing a picture and so am I with you. I am playing with you in a way you can tolerate." They wanted to create a felt sense for Luke, "You see me, you can handle my big feelings." They also began to draw characters that might be able to play with his monster, join his monster, help his monster. They did not know exactly what would work, but they began with the intention of being present and creating safety and over time wanting to scaffold him to find new ways to handle the monster in his play.

The Teachers Share How Play Progressed for Them with Luke

Teacher Wendi. "I remember this one particular instance of Luke drawing a monster again, very intense looking and blood and weapons and these pokey things on the monster, and I decided to draw a big soft monster on a separate paper and wondered with Luke, "What if my monster wants to give your monster a hug?" And he would respond, "My monster will poke it with its pokes." And I said, "Well, I think that's OK. I think I can tolerate being poked a little. Do you think your monster could maybe hold hands if yours does not want a hug?" The goal was just to move toward an option where Luke's monster could be nice and safe and that hugging or holding hands could also be safe, but it could be from monster to monster.

Teacher Huan. "Previously, we all saw his drawings and were really worried for him and afraid. We thought his drawings meant that he was thinking about violence all the time. When, in fact, now I understand that he was sharing how scared and terrified he was and is. For much of his life he hasn't had language to state this. So, he needed someone to literally 'sit in his fear with him.' One day when I was sitting with him and he was drawing a monster, I drew a friendly monster and asked his monster, "Can I play with you today?" At first, he just ignored my monster but when I could see that he was able to manage it, I gently offered again and then said, "You look nice. I would like to play with you when you are ready. I am building blocks and a tower. Let me know, Luke, if you ever want to play and I will be ready."

Teacher Pato. "I think that was a really a powerful place when we met as a team to think together and ask, 'How do we join Luke?' 'How do we build our ability to be able to witness something so painful for this little person, so he doesn't feel alone?' I will never forget how after 3 months of using these new strategies, I was sitting with Luke but I was not drawing anything. Then he grabbed a piece of paper and crayons and put them in front of me. He pointed to my paper. I realized (almost with tears of joy in my eyes) he was inviting me to play. This was his invitation to connect. This is what healing looks like. He had a desire to play with me, so he extended an invitation. After he did this, I drew a monster and asked, "Would you like to play with me today? We could draw our favorite thing to play with in our picture." He drew a dog and so I drew one. Then I made a comment, "Our doggies are friends and can play together. We can find a bone and bury it. We can chase a ball together." Then he drew a doggie and I drew some grass with a bone buried in the dirt for his dog to find. The best part of the story was when he smiled and laughed as he lifted up his paper to make his dog pretend to find the bone I drew.

Rose reflected on her time with the teachers in this classroom. "As a therapist and mental health consultant, I recognize that my job is different and even when there is heaviness, I am there for several hours while teachers are there in it all day, every day, with Luke. They are heroes to me. They have the most power to rewire the stress response system of a child. This child, the teachers, their relationship, it was really beautiful. Part of my work was to give the teachers a time and place to acknowledge their pain witnessing this child. And also, to name how many competing pressures they are under at all times. We have to honor them with tenderness and with grace. Being able to name some of that provided an opportunity for the teachers to feel seen and understood. And I tried to remain honest and humble as I worked with them. I named how painful it was for me to witness this child's experience, to hear about it, to see it in his play. I named these feelings without going into detail that some of it brought up very painful and personal experiences that I could relate to.

I wasn't asking them to do therapy with me, but I was asking them to think about whether some of the strong emotions Luke is bringing up for them might be due to their own backgrounds and trauma. Was his story touching something in them? Some pain from their own lives? I always emphasize the importance of caring about each other—directly supporting each other and, when appropriate, encouraging each other to get outside support. This work is so heavy when you really sit in it. One of the most important things early childhood teachers can do is to bear witness to children's pain and to hold hope that we can make a positive difference for the child with each and every interaction. The most difficult skill we all have to learn—especially for adults with histories of trauma—is to stop trying to reactively jump in and try to 'fix it or make it better' to reduce our own feelings of discomfort."

Reflection/Discussion Questions

- ◆ Where do you get support inside and outside work so that you have a space to regularly reflect, pause, and to keep your cortex open so that your amygdala and hindbrain do not hijack you to react fast?
- ◆ Have you ever pulled yourself back from jumping in to try and fix a child's problem or to make the child feel better when witnessing painful expressions in play? Can you imagine instead bearing witness and attuning to their story as a form of healing for the child?

Teachers maintaining their own support, self-care, and self-awareness is important in working with trauma-impacted children—teachers who are able to regulate, problem solve, and have restored energy to deal with witnessing the painful stories the children share through their play. We also learned that when we jump in to fix or cheer a child up, we are communicating to them, "I don't want to know, I can't look at it, and I just want you to be happy, and in my classroom you are only allowed to share stories in your play with happy endings."

References

Bishop, R. S. (1990). Mirrors, windows, and sliding glass doors. Originally published in *Perspectives*, 1(3), ix–xi. Retrieved from https://scenicregional. org/wp-content/uploads/2017/08/Mirrors-Windows-and-Sliding-Glass-Doors.pdf

Conkbayir, M. (2017). *Early childhood and neuroscience: Theory, research and implications for practice*. New York, NY: Bloomsbury Academic.

Ghosh Ippen, C. (2017). *Once I was very very scared*. San Francisco, CA: Piplo Productions.

Landreth, G. (2002). *Play therapy: The art of relationship* (2nd ed.). New York, NY: Brunner-Routledge.

Miranda, L. M. (2021). We don't talk about Bruno. *Encanto*. Walt Disney Records.

Nicholson, J., Driscoll, P., Kurtz, J., Wesley, L., & Benitez, D. (2019). *Culturally responsive self-care practices for early childhood educators*. New York, NY: Routledge.

Pattakos, A., & Dundon, E. (2017). *Prisoners of our thoughts: Viktor Frankl's principles for discovering meaning in life and work* (3rd ed.). Oakland, CA: Berrett-Koehler.

Rushton, S. (2011). Neuroscience, early childhood education and play: We are doing it right! *Early Childhood Education Journal*, 39(2), 89–94. doi: 10.1007/ s10643-011-0447-z

Shamoon-Shanok, R. (2006). Reflective supervision for an integrated model. In G. M. Foley & J. D. Hochman (Eds.), *Mental health in early intervention: Achieving unity in principles and practice* (pp. 343–381). Baltimore, MD: Brookes.

Siegel, D., & Payne Bryson, T. (2012). *The whole-brain child: 12 revolutionary strategies to nurture your child's developing mind.* London: Bantam Books.

Wolfe, P. (2007). *Mind, memory and learning: Translating brain research to classroom practices.* Napa Valley, CA: Association for Supervision and Curriculum Development (ASCD).

2

Building Consistent, Attuned, and Responsive Relationships with Young Children through Play

Building consistent, attuned, and responsive relationships is the essential investment early educators need to make to support children experiencing stress and trauma. Tuning in to the child's perspective begins by taking time to mindfully focus on the child and show genuine interest in understanding what their emotional state and/or behavior is communicating through their play. Attunement is characterized by careful observation of children and responding to children's complex, puzzling, or challenging behavior by asking, what story is this child communicating to me about how they feel and what they need to feel safe? Attunement is supported when adults focus in on a child's emotional state, verbalizations, and/or non-verbal expressions and behavior without judgment or reactivity but instead respond with interest, curiosity, empathy, and a desire to provide support.

    With attuned relational interactions, trust forms and feelings of safety are increased for the child, which can positively influence

DOI: 10.4324/9781003326113-3

the child's ability to be in the optimal zone of arousal (regulation) and to have capacity to engage in learning.

What is Affect Attunement? What Does it Mean to Engage in Emotionally Attuned Interactions with a Young Child?

Affect attunement (Stern, 1985) is an interactive process that involves a teacher monitoring and regulating their own internal emotional state and behavior in order to communicate messages of calm, care, and safety to a young distressed child. By maintaining their own self-regulation, the educator supports the child to calm their nervous system (Schore, 2005). When a teacher "attunes" to a child in this way and responds to a child's feelings of distress with caring, calm, and supportive messages, they help the child develop self-regulation skills and a healthy stress response system (Schore, 2003, 2005). In contrast, an adult who responds reactively (e.g., punish, blame, consequences, threats, ignore) to children's distress will increase their stress, which can further disorganize their nervous systems and increase their emotional and behavioral dysregulation (Schuder & Lyons-Ruth, 2004). Educators who do not respond to children's distress with calm and regulated behavior will actually intensify children's traumatic stress and leave young children with the impression that adults will not be available to support them in their times of need (Nicholson, Kurtz, Perez, Bryant, & Giles, 2023).

Attunement creates what van der Kolk (2014) describes as a *visceral feeling of safety*:

> Social support is not the same as merely being in the presence of others. The critical issue is reciprocity— being truly heard and seen by the people around us, feeling that we are held in someone else's mind and heart. *For our physiology to calm down, heal, and grow we need a visceral feeling of safety.*
>
> (p. 79; emphasis added)

On the importance of consistency and responsiveness, Jeanie Liang, a child life specialist working with children who have undergone heart surgery, shares:

> Realize for a lot of these children impacted by trauma sometimes it's about showing up, it's about coming back, it's about being consistent. Many of these children are impacted by too much uncertainty and a lack of predictability. So showing up and holding that *safe and predictable space* can literally just be the greatest gift we can give them. When it's in the context of play, I think it's also *being present* and not always having an active, directive or teaching role. But it can be opening yourself up to listen to the child and all of their senses, and how they're interacting with the world in their play, and with you, and being able to meet the child where they are.

Image of the Child

Loris Malaguzzi (1994), early childhood educator and founder of the Reggio Emilia approach, reinforced how the way we treat children is significantly impacted by our *"image of the child."* This phrase refers to our cultural understandings and assumptions about the role of children in education and society. Every culture has its own set of expectations and beliefs about children—what we believe children are capable of, what motivates them, how much agency or autonomy in decision making and actions children should have, and our goals for their learning and development (Rogoff, 2003). Our "image of the child" is influenced by our diverse social connections, cultural and family beliefs, and the historical contexts of our communities. Malaguzzi explains:

> There are hundreds of different images of the child. Each one of you has inside yourself an image of the child that directs you as you begin to relate to a child. This theory within you pushes you to behave in certain ways;

it orients you as you talk to the child, listen to the child, observe the child. It is very difficult for you to act contrary to this internal image.

(p. 52)

Our image of the child influences the way we relate to children and the way we design early learning environments (California Department of Education, Early Education Division, 2021). The decisions we make about curriculum and instruction, classroom management, assessment and communication with parents and families are all rooted in our cultural assumptions, values, and beliefs about the image of the child, especially how children learn and develop, and what we believe the role of adults and peers in children's learning and development to be.

Constructing an Image of the Child Impacted by Trauma

Children must be understood to be complex human beings and not solely defined by the trauma they experience. A central foundation of high-quality early childhood education is using a strengths-based (versus deficit orientation) perspective in discussions of children and their families, and this remains true in discussions of early childhood trauma. This is why our discussion about trauma is always balanced with a consideration of the "whole child" and the topics of resiliency and healing. It is essential to acknowledge that all children are complex individuals and have many aspects of their lives. When we talk about the "whole child" we are including consideration of children's *diverse*:

- ◆ Relationships
- ◆ Family, cultural, and community values and beliefs, routines, rituals, experiences, and memories
- ◆ Aspects of identity (race, ethnicity, gender, primary language, ability, etc.)
- ◆ Interests, likes/dislikes

- Temperaments
- Personalities
- Protective factors
- Support systems
- Strengths inherent in the child and that surround the child (Nicholson, Perez, & Kurtz, 2019).

Be aware of labeling or stigmatizing children as "traumatized." It is important not to construct an image of a young child that defines them by the trauma they have experienced. Trauma may be a significant and impactful feature of their life; however, it does not represent all of the complex aspects of who they are. This type of deficit language does not recognize the resources, personal characteristics, and relationships available to support the child to cope, heal, and even to thrive. It is important to perceive every child as having a range of strengths, assets, skills, interests, and vulnerabilities.

Every child needs somebody to be their biggest fan. Someone who will notice them and take time to build a relationship with them. This doesn't mean it always has to be the classroom teacher. Sometimes we feel guilty about the fact that we are not able to connect with every child. We're human and sometimes we might find it difficult to build a relationship with a specific child and that's OK. When this happens, think about who else within your classroom or school might be able to connect with that child and be their biggest fan. It could be a co-teacher or the teacher in the classroom across the playground. It might be the custodian or the person who serves lunch each day; it just needs to be someone that can be that child's biggest fan. It's so important that we are mindful of this.

(Brulene Zanutto, young learner administrator)

Be willing to acknowledge the reality of trauma even if it makes you uncomfortable to do so. Though we don't want to overly emphasize trauma in our image of a child, it is also important that we don't ignore children's adverse experiences. It is very difficult for adults to acknowledge that so many young and vulnerable children experience trauma. Thinking about infants, toddlers, preschool and elementary school children in pain, harmed, terrified—and far too often, as a result of the actions of their own parents and caregivers—is a reality that too many adults do not want to confront. To reduce their anxiety and discomfort, many adults create an image of the child as being too young to remember their traumatic experiences or as "naturally resilient" in the face of adversity. As we discuss in this book, neither of these assumptions is accurate. To the contrary, brain research highlights that children are the most vulnerable and impacted by trauma. Even trauma endured in utero impacts young children's developing brains and bodies and can cause lasting damage throughout a child's life.

Trauma-sensitive early childhood programs validate *all* children's life experiences, including the large percentage of children who experience trauma in their earliest years. Trauma-responsive early childhood programs and systems do not ignore or understate the painful and authentic realities of the widespread existence of trauma in children's lives. Bearing witness to children's pain and suffering without blaming or judging them for these experiences, and accurately and honestly acknowledging the consequences of trauma's impact, is a foundational principle of all trauma-responsive work with young children. As Landreth (2002) reminds us, "Children are people, they are capable of experiencing deep emotional pain and joy" (p. 54).

Reflect on your "Ideal" Image of a Child

Cultural values, perceptions, and beliefs shape each adult's expectations for young children—what we think they are capable of, our beliefs about how children should behave, what the role of adults is in children's learning and development, and how much agency and control we believe children should have in their learning process. These unconscious images impact the way we relate to children and our decisions about arranging learning environments for them.

Think of a young child you know and/or work with who displays stress-related behaviors and/or is impacted by trauma:

◆ What language (words, phrases, metaphors) do you use when you talk about this child? What stories do you typically tell about this child?

◆ How might your language influence what you think and how you feel about this child? How do you and/or others interact with and treat this child?

◆ How might this child be internalizing your beliefs, attitudes, and judgments about them? How might the stories you tell about them influence their developing sense of belonging and identity? Their felt sense of safety or danger in your presence?

It is important to bring to conscious awareness our "ideal image of a child," including images of how we view children who have experienced trauma. These images can impact how we respond to children in both positive and harmful ways.

It is so important for the adults in the system to make the children feel like they are seen. It sounds so simple, yet it can truly make a positive difference. Small actions can really add up to have a big impact. Using the child's name and pronouncing it correctly, looking them in the eye when you talk with them, remembering something they told you and then remembering to ask about it the next time you see them. These may seem like like things, and yet in the life of a child, whether that child is 5 years old or 15, these simple actions can mean so much and really show the child that they are seen.

(Brulene Zanutto, Young Learners' Program specialist)

Shifting from "What is Wrong with You?" to "What is Your Behavior Communicating?"

How can we give a child a voice who otherwise does not have one or who has lost it due to trauma and toxic stress?

A young child does not yet have the fully developed skillset to identify how they feel and to express themselves with words, so their dysregulated behavior communicates a story. The first reaction most of us have when faced with a child's puzzling behavior is, "What is wrong with you?" This perspective leads to reactions that are trauma-inducing, such as punishment, consequences, ignoring, blaming, or bribing. We can build a trauma-responsive muscle to be a "detective" or careful observer of children's behavior. A trauma-responsive perspective would be, "What is your story? Or, what is your behavior communicating to me?" This allows us to cultivate a pause so that we can respond to children with empathy, compassion, and a belief that there is meaning behind the child's dysregulated behavior. This perspective helps us see that all behavior and the trauma-related stories they share through their play are forms of communication.

This *reframe (What is your behavior communicating?)* gives us a context for the behavior, fosters connection and compassion, and helps us to see the hidden strengths that children are bringing to protect them in the face of adversity with their dysregulated behavior. It allows us to pause before we react in ways that are threatening, bribing, shaming, including yelling and ignoring to try to stop the behavior. Those reactionary behaviors can cause more harm to children with trauma histories as they frighten them even more: they do not promote safety nor do they support children to learn to identify their emotions, recognize when their emotions are too big to handle, or learn ways to calm and regulate their oversize emotions. When we take this stance of "What is your behavior communicating?" instead of "What is wrong with you?" we support children with histories of trauma and toxic stress to feel safe. When we move our own internal voice from "What is wrong with you?" to "What is your behavior communicating?" we are supporting children to have a voice *and* to be heard.

Rose Tandeta, a child life specialist, uses play to understand how children are coping with hospitalization, and as a tool for children to express their feelings. She offered the following questions to help people who work with young children get curious instead of jumping to solid conclusions. She asks herself these questions while the play is happening, and when she is reflecting back on the play:

1. What is happening with rules and who makes the decisions (following, breaking, inventing, etc.)?
2. Is there frustration or calm for the child?
3. What themes are emerging (filling, dumping, transporting, collecting, isolating, etc.)?
4. How are they using the materials and which materials are they drawn to or avoiding?
5. Is there a quality of "stuck-ness" in their play?
6. Are they playing out experiences you know they've had?
7. Is there engagement with others, with me? Are attempts being made to engage with others?

Daniel and the Teachers Collaborate to Support Alex

Daniel Nieves Rivera is a mental health specialist at a social services organization with 15 years of experience working in the field. He provides mental health services to children, teachers, and families for several programs. Daniel shares a story about a young child who has experienced trauma and how he supports the teachers in moving their collective voices from "What is wrong with you?" to "What is your behavior communicating?"

Alex is a 4-year-old child who lives with his dad, Jose, and two older sisters, Arya and Angelica. Alex and his family have gone through Child Protective Services (CPS) as Alex's mom was reported as being physically abusive to Alex and his siblings. At school, Alex exhibits disruptive behaviors. Over several classroom observations Daniel recognizes that it's hard for Alex to regulate and slow down. He knocks overs blocks children are building, takes toys away from other children, runs and throws toys at children, while smiling and looking at the teachers. When a child takes a toy that Alex is using, he screams and hits. Transitions are also challenging for Alex as he tends to run around the classroom with little focus or ability to stay on task. Alex doesn't talk at school; rather he points, makes humming sounds, and gestures with his head for affirmation and denial. When the teaching team shares this with his dad Jose, he responds that Alex speaks in complete sentences at home. He explains that after school, while they walk to the bus station, Alex talks to him about the things that happened at school. Jose records a video of Alex talking about the things he learned at school; for example, counting from one to ten and naming different colors.

Children who have experienced trauma live in bodies that are turned on "high alert." Their brain and body continually operate in "survival" mode (flight, freeze, or fight) to protect them from memories that are connected to past trauma and that they perceive in the present moment as threatening. When they persistently experience traumatic events, their body can be rewired to be in a hyper-aroused (fight or flight) or hypo-aroused state (freeze) all day. Additionally, because they are rarely in the zone of optimal arousal and their cortex is closed, and because they are preoccupied with survival, they then have difficulty with the age-appropriate skills that other children, coming from safe environments with nurturing relationships, may have developed.

Daniel meets with the teachers to support them to share their observations of Alex and to brainstorm ideas about the specific strategies they can use to support him. The teachers' initial response to Alex's behavior is that "he is doing things on purpose." The teachers default to this common survival response when they feel helpless and can't find a strategy to support a child with Alex's behavior. Daniel guides the teachers to look deeper into Alex's dysregulated behavior to understand that Alex's actions have meaning and when he throws toys at children, it may be his way of getting children's attention or signaling that he wants to play with them. Underneath, he suggests, Alex's behavior could also be communicating that he has a desire to connect. Another interpretation is that Alex might be seeking teachers' reactions to see how they respond, providing information to his body to discern if the adults are safe for him in order to build trust.

When a teacher's voice stops at *"What is wrong with you?"* the trajectory of their reactions can be blaming, shaming, consequences, threats, punishment, ignoring, or exclusionary practices.

When a teacher's voice moves to *"What happened to you?"* their behavior moves from reactive to one of more curiosity and empathy. They seek to understand what may have happened to the child.

When a teacher's voice moves to *"What is the meaning behind your behavior?"* they move even farther to a trauma-responsive approach by seeking to understand what the child's puzzling behavior is communicating.

Daniel was trying to cultivate a pause to allow the teachers to access the third trauma-responsive voice and to seek what the meaning of Alex's behavior was communicating.

The teaching team reflects on the meaning behind Alex's behavior and they decide to *focus on helping him build relational connections with others.* In taking time to reflect about his behavior, they realized he had difficulty engaging with his peers appropriately. He wanted to have a connection with others, but he entered play or responded to invitations to play with awkward, abrupt, and aggressive responses. Here is an example of two practices the teacher used to begin to help Alex develop friendship skills.

Daniel first spent time playing with Alex. He would play games to promote connection, social interaction, and emotional regulation. During the play, he would guide Alex how to practice the following:

- ◆ How to ask if you can join play, "Can I play with you?" and ask a teacher to be his "voice" for the moment
- ◆ How to handle when he does not get his way, strategies to regulate, and asking teachers to practice co-regulation skills when he is upset and redirection

◆ How to tell others when you don't want to play (e.g., encouraging him to gesture with the hand and say "stop").

Next, Daniel would engage him in parallel play with activities he really likes close to another child (e.g., water table, sand table, building a structure, or playing with car toys). He would say, "Alex, should we invite Michael to play with us today?" "Should we practice some things we have been learning together about play?" In these small ways, he was able to facilitate play for Alex so he could develop enough trust to be able to connect with peers and caregivers. Because Alex was seeking connection in unhealthy ways, this helped him get what he needed in healthy and appropriate ways.

Daniel and the Teachers Collaborate to Support Alex's Family

Another important element of Daniel's collaboration with the teachers is to intentionally work to build *trust and strengthen the relationship with Alex's dad*. Daniel knows that this will not be an easy task as Jose is a single parent of three children and he himself has gone through trauma. He is quiet and reserved and does not typically communicate much with any of the school staff. Yet, Daniel has made a positive connection with Jose. He explains: "Maybe because of the connection we share with our cultural background, we developed a relationship. He is Latino, I am Latino, so we spoke in Spanish." Once Daniel and Jose had built this connection, Jose began to open up and share his reasons for not being more open and asking for help for Alex. He shares, *"I'm afraid that CPS will take him."* Daniel and the team support Jose by focusing on his strengths, reassuring and acknowledging all the positive things he is doing: he is a diligent, hard-working father who brings his children to school every day and brushes his daughters' hair. This connection helps Jose become more open to services and therapy for Alex.

Daniel's Role in Supporting the Teachers

Daniel perceives a few things that consistently come up as struggles for the teachers. He knows that the tendency to label a child can be another way the teachers are saying, "I am really overwhelmed, I am really frustrated, I don't feel I have the support I need." Given this, Daniel supports the teachers in a few important ways:

◆ The first thing Daniel does is to work on *building trust with the teachers by creating a safe space to resonate with their experience*. He starts with teacher reflection, creating a time and space for the teachers to express their feelings about working with Alex. He notices that when the teachers have a safe space to meet and talk, they share the experience and feelings that they have been holding in. Daniel starts by inviting teachers to share how they feel, and he prioritizes active listening with compassion. He recognizes that in the beginning it may look like venting with strong reactions and judgments about the child and family. But with time, the teachers become more regulated and are open to exploring new possibilities and considerations. Before they were so burned out that they could not even think about anything other than their own intense feelings. Daniel explains, "Teachers just want to be listened to; they want to express their frustration in a safe environment where they are respected. I want to provide them with those spaces and to build trusting relationships with the teachers, so they have a place to express their emotions."

◆ After taking this time to support the teachers to be able to vent and feel heard and supported, Daniel then *guides the teachers to build empathy for Alex*. He focuses on helping them "see" some of Alex's strengths, such as resilience, playfulness, willingness to learn, contagious smile, enjoyment building structures with peers, calmness when playing with sand or water, and his expressions of affection (e.g., hugging teachers and leaning his head into their shoulders after teachers help him regulate).

◆ Daniel first supported teachers in expressing and regulating their feelings and this helped the teachers to access more empathy and compassion for Alex. They were then able to *problem solve and to explore the meaning behind Alex's behavior* and identify concrete trauma-responsive practices that could support Alex in feeling safe and building relational connections.

◆ In addition, Daniel stated a curious fact about Alex. At the end of school, to the surprise of everyone in the school, Alex began to verbalize his experience very clearly and using complete sentences. He was engaging with teachers and school staff, talking about the new school and his sisters. On repeated occasions Alex said in his native language Spanish: "I'm going to my sisters' school." Daniel expressed, "Alex seemed very happy. That sense of isolation, traumatic reactions, and his difficulty verbalizing words at school were gone at that moment. We can attribute this result to many different reasons, although we believe the integration and development of factors such as empathy with teachers, connections with dad, trust, playfulness, healthy relationships, and our team effort played an important role in this case not only for Alex but everyone around him."

Spotlight on a Trauma-Responsive Practice: Disrupting Reactivity through Reflection

An essential trauma-responsive practice Daniel is using is to support the teachers to disrupt their reactivity by helping them to slow down and learn to use reflection. *Reflection moves people from being reactive* (punishing, blaming, bribing) *towards being responsive and seeking to understand the meaning underneath the dysregulating behavior* that is disrupting the classroom environment and others. Once the teachers identified the meaning of the behavior (e.g., Alex was seeking connection but did not have the skill), they were able to support a plan to teach Alex new skills such as how to play with others. Alex could only be taught this skill when his cortex was open for business, and he was regulated. That is why they started by playing with Daniel to calm his stress response system. After practice and over time, Daniel was able to focus on developing more complex skills by inviting other children into Alex's play with his support.

This story highlights *the power of the parallel process*. Daniel treated the teachers the way we want teachers to treat the child. When Daniel responded by listening, having empathy and compassion for the teachers' feelings, they had a pathway to regulate big emotions that were hijacking their hindbrain/survival brain to be reactive and judgmental (e.g., he is doing this on purpose). Once the teachers were calm and regulated through this reflective support, they had the restored energy and access to their executive functioning skills required to think and reason and problem solve for the greater good of the child and family. They pivoted from being reactive to being responsive by seeking the meaning of Alex's behavior.

Reflection/Discussion Questions

Giving every child a voice requires an intentional moment to pause, to reflect, to regulate, to reason so that we strive to move our first reactionary voice from "What is wrong with you?" to a trauma-responsive voice, "What is your behavior communicating?"

◆ What is one strategy you can use in the moment when you are with a child who is dysregulated, so that you cultivate a "pause and regulate," so that you open your cortex to explore "What might the child's dysregulated behavior be communicating they need?"?
◆ It is common for adults who have a child with challenges in the classroom to jump to the conclusion that they originate in the family. This frame can adversely impact how we relate to families. Have you ever paused that voice of

blame and instead responded by seeking advice, support, and collaboration from the child's family?

Building Responsive Relationships with Young Children: A Felt Sense of Safety is the Foundation

Building on our image of the child, turn back to the focus of this chapter, which is building consistent, attuned, and responsive relationships with children. The number-one pathway to buffer the stress of a trauma-impacted child is a calm, attuned, and nurturing caregiver. In this first vignette we will observe the presence of a regulated adult who understands that this child can borrow their calm to regulate their activated nervous system.

"I am Just Going to Sit Nearby"

Lindsay, a preschool teacher, shares about Katie, a young 4-year-old in her classroom who ran under a table to hide and started to shake and lose her ability to talk. Lindsay recognized in that moment that she did not need to know "why," she just needed to do whatever it would take to help Katie to feel safe.

> There was a 4-year-old child in my classroom and her name was Katie. When Katie got upset, she would run [flight] under a table in the classroom and start to shake and lose all ability to listen or talk [freeze]. We never knew if Katie had a trauma history. In fact, I attended a trauma training and the trainer said that we don't need to know the trauma history to help a child. The trainer said that trauma-responsive practices align with all social-emotional trainings and that they are good for all kids. But I do remember the trainer saying one big thing…that the primary goal is to help children feel safe with me, in my classroom and in the moment.
>
> I thought to myself, "What will help this child feel safe in this very moment? Katie must be frightened

since she ran to hide under a table and started shaking."
I slowly approached Katie and said to her in a quiet and
calm voice, "*I am just going to sit nearby.*" I learned that
quickly approaching Katie or entering her space abruptly
dysregulated her even more. It was hard because I wanted
to hug her, but I reminded myself that a central foundation of trauma-responsive practice is helping the child to
feel safe with me. So, I softly said to Katie, "I am going to
sit near you. I'm here if you want to come sit closer to me
or you need some help." I also said, "Katie, when you are
ready, I am right here."

Then I just sat there for what felt like several
minutes and then I moved my body slightly closer to
the table, saying, "I am going to come a bit closer in
case you want me to hear what you are saying." Katie
stayed quiet for another few minutes. I moved my hand
so that Katie could reach it if she wanted to. After about
a minute, she reached out to my hand and grabbed it.
After another minute, I then said, "May I come in?"
Katie scooted back and allowed me to sit under the
table with her. I was glad that I had learned to manage
my own protective urge to rush in too quickly to try to
comfort her. Taking the approach I did—that is, saying
very little and moving very slowly and allowing Katie
to remain in control regarding my physical proximity
to her—strengthened her felt sense of safety in my
presence which helped her feel a greater sense of trust
in our relationship.

Trauma-Responsive Practices that Teacher Lindsay was Using to Support Katie to Feel Safe

◆ *Calmness is contagious.* Trauma-responsive practice is
understanding that being in the presence of a caring
adult can immediately calm the sensory response system
of a child.

◆ *Prosody and tone of voice and non-verbal body language
send a message of safety.* Using a gentle tone of voice and
non-verbal body clues that convey calm, co-regulatory

support helps children who are experiencing stress to feel safe.

♦ *Individualizing strategies based on what the child can tolerate.* These include resisting the urge to rush in and over-whelm a child's stress response system; understanding that Katie needs adults to approach her slowly; and recognizing that just being nearby and present can help her feel safe.

♦ *Control and choice.* This can mean giving a child a sense of control and choice: "When you are ready, you let me know" and "I will ask your permission to move closer." This strategy provides the child with a felt sense of safety because the message they receive is, "You are asking permission and I am in charge of my body and the space around it."

♦ *Calming the hindbrain before engaging the cortex.* This means reducing the amount of talking, directing, or throwing out solutions that are a teacher's best attempt to help the child feel better. Recognizing when the cortex is shut down that a silent presence that conveys "I am here and you are safe" is more powerful for Katie than words filled with directions.

Building Responsive Relationships with Young Children: A Felt Sense of Belonging

Trauma is not all of who I am, but it is a part of me. When I bring it into my play in the classroom and you listen, when you are curious about what I feel and have experienced, I relax knowing that at least one adult sees me, is not scared, and helps me feel a sense of belonging, even if there are parts that feel scary to you.

(Julie Kurtz)

In the following vignette Teacher Karen shows us how she supports a child named Preeta to have a felt sense of belonging as a key part of building attuned and responsive relationships. It involves providing for the child a sense of belonging that allows them to be authentic and not to receive messages that they have to hide parts of themselves or their lived experiences. This includes allowing them to bring in the "hard stuff" without trying to shut them down or look away.

Grandma Can Give Them a Hug

Teacher Karen Galicia, a social-emotional specialist working in a Head Start program, explains that when children play with toys, early educators can seize opportunities to talk about their feelings and/or how they're doing emotionally in the moment. Preeta, a 4-year-old girl in Karen's classroom, recently experienced the death of her father. Karen shares a story of how Preeta began to express her feelings through play. When Preeta played with the dolls she would say, "The doll died," or "He's dead." Here is an example of one conversation that unfolded during play with Preeta where the theme of death came up:

> Preeta was playing with four dolls: two adult-like figures and two children. She was creating an imaginary scene in a house. The family was eating dinner.
>
> **Preeta:** Oh no, he is dead.
> **Teacher Karen:** Who is dead?
> **Preeta:** It is the dad. He is dead.
> **Teacher Karen:** What does dead mean, Preeta?
> **Preeta:** It means you don't come back. You can't eat any more. You won't live at your home with your kids. You are in heaven.
> **Teacher Karen:** How does this doll feel [pointing to the adult doll who is not dead]?
> **Preeta:** She cries a lot and is sad.
> **Teacher Karen:** She is sad because this doll is in heaven and won't live at home any longer?
> **Preeta:** [Nods yes.]

Teacher Karen: And how does this doll feel [pointing to young child doll]?

Preeta: Sad.

Teacher Karen: It is OK for the dolls to feel sad. When we love someone and they die, it can feel very sad. When the dolls talk about how they feel it can help them when they feel big feelings of sadness. What are some things the dolls can do to feel safe and help when they feel sad?

Preeta: Ask for a hug.

Teacher Karen: Yes, a hug can help. Is there someone who can help the dolls who feel sad by giving them a hug?

Preeta: This doll over there is the grandma. She can come in and give them a hug.

Teacher Karen: That sounds like a great idea. Let's have grandma come in and give them all a hug.

Teacher Karen is taking the child's lead and making sure not to push Preeta too far out of her zone of optimal regulation. She is making sure not to lead her with statements such as, "That must feel scary" or "They must be scared." She also wants to make sure to not suggest where a person (or doll) goes after they die as children and families have many different beliefs and ways of talking about death. She follows the child's lead. Therefore, she used the word heaven because Preeta had shared that the doll had died and was now in heaven. Teacher Karen repeated back what Preeta had said. She asked her a simple question building on what Preeta said (e.g., How did doll X feel?). She waits to see if Preeta can tolerate that curious question while staying regulated. More importantly, by Teacher Karen being a trusted adult who is present in the moment, listening to Preeta's feelings and acknowledging her experience, she is creating a safe space for Preeta to express the loss of and sadness about her father. Attuned relational presence from an adult who shows compassion and curiosity is one of the strongest pathways to help a child feel a sense of belonging and to buffer children's stress during traumatic events. Further, Preeta is receiving messages that she is accepted and that all parts of her are honored even when she has "hard stuff" she shows from her life. She doesn't have to have shame and hide that part of herself from the teachers.

Reflection/Discussion Questions

◆ Can you recall a time when you worked with a child who experienced something scary, and it came out through their play? Have you tried one of the trauma-responsive practices that we observed Karen using with Preeta:
   • Attuned relational presence without fixing or offering solutions to feel better or be happy?
   • Listening and repeating back what you hear so that the child feels seen and heard and has a safe space to express their feelings?

Building Responsive Relationships with Young Children: Close Connections with Families

A unique and essential aspect of early childhood is building partnerships with parents and families (Nicholson & Kurtz, 2021). Our commitment to these relationships is to remain present and attuned to families even when they are struggling. Being trauma-responsive is not looking the other way or avoiding difficult topics but, instead, being available for the children and families we are serving.

In the story below we learn from teacher Sal that building relationships with children includes prioritizing the relationship with their family members. Although this is an emotionally challenging situation for the child, teacher, and family, Sal teaches us that with a caring collaboration between the teacher and the family we can all work in the best interest of the child.

"I Love You, Mom. I Want You Not to Be Sick"

Sal Mana has been a preschool teacher for almost 14 years and is currently working at an urban Head Start program. He shares a story of how he and his team supported a child who was experiencing one of the most stressful experiences a child could have—the terminal illness of a parent.

Martin started the school at 2 years and stayed in the program until he was 4½. He lives with his mom Camila. Five months before transitioning to kindergarten Martin's mom got cancer. Before his mom got sick, Martin was a happy child who loved playing with cars and drawing monsters and was very kind to his friends. Then suddenly, this stressful event happened in his life. At the beginning, Camila seemed to be doing fine but little by little, she started to change. She lost a lot of weight, had spots on her hands, and whenever she would drop off Martin to school she would stay longer because Martin would get very emotional. And not only that, but Martin's behavior started to change. Martin knew his mom was sick because she told him. Camila explained that she has cancer and that means you are sick for a long time. When she got spots on her hands, she told Martin that's from being sick. So now during drop offs, Martin would just sit and rub her hand and only wanted to be close to her. During his play, he became very aggressive. He would not share. If someone wanted to play with him, he would say no or hit them. He did not want to transition when the group would go outside or clean up after play. There were moments when he would start yelling because he didn't want to do a transition.

Teacher Sal tried to support him by reading books about emotions, such as *When I Miss You* by Cornelia Maude Spelman. Other times it was a book that Martin would pick from the classroom library. Sal would spend time with Martin, trying to involve him in play by providing materials and engaging himself in the activity as well. He would take out the cars that Martin liked, hoping that that might cheer him up. But Martin often refused to engage. When that happened, the teacher would say, "I'll just sit here with you. And I will be here if you need me." Most times, Martin and the teacher would just sit next to each other. Eventually, after about 10 minutes Martin would stop crying but he would still refuse to interact or play.

The teachers knew that he also enjoyed drawing, so they provided him with opportunities to express himself through art. Most times he would draw his mom and make cards for her. In fact, he would make ten cards every day. The cards were covered in scribbles but for Martin they were powerful words and hopes. Some cards would say "I love you, mom," "I want you not to be sick," and he would draw pictures of them both playing at the park. Occasionally, he would play with the other children but then he would say, "I need to make another card for my mom." When mom would come to pick him up, he would say, "Mama, I made a card for you. It says I love you!" Mom shared that at home he would often open the cards and read them to her: "Dear mom, I want you to feel better."

Teacher Sal understood that Martin needed to spend more time with his mother. Together with Camila they came up with a plan where mom would stay longer during drop offs so that Martin could feel some comfort. They would read books together and play with toys. To prepare Martin for her departure, she would tell him that just before washing hands and sitting for breakfast she would give him a hug and then leave. Knowing that Martin needed to spend more time with her, Sal and Camila also agreed that every couple of weeks she would come at lunchtime to sit with him and eat lunch. The last month she would come in every day and that helped Martin because he knew that he didn't have to stay a whole day without seeing her.

Reflection/Discussion Question

♦ Some teachers fear the longer drop off will create more emotion and a more difficult drop-off routine. Why do you think that this routine of taking more time with his mom at drop off helped Martin and eased the emotional intensity of his reaction after mom left in the morning?

References

California Department of Education, Early Education Division (2021). *The powerful role of play in education: Birth–8*. Retrieved from www.cde.ca.gov/sp/cd/re/documents/powerfulroleofplay.pdf

Landreth, G. (2002). *Play therapy: The art of relationship* (2nd ed.). New York, NY: Brunner-Routledge.

Malaguzzi, L. (1994). Your image of the child: Where teaching begins. *Childcare Exchange*. Retrieved from www.reggioalliance.org/downloarvardguzzi:ccie:1994.pdf

Nicholson, J., & Kurtz, J. (2021). *Trauma-responsive family engagement in early childhood: Practices for equity and resilience*. New York, NY: Routledge.

Nicholson, J., Perez, L., & Kurtz, J. (2019). *Trauma-informed practices for early childhood educators: Relationship-based approaches that support healing and build resilience in young children*. New York, NY: Routledge.

Nicholson, J., Kurtz, J., Perez, L., Bryant, S., & Giles, D. (2023). *Trauma-informed practices for early childhood educators: Relationship-based approaches that support healing and build resilience in young children* (2nd ed.). New York, NY: Routledge.

Rogoff, B. (2003). *The cultural nature of human development*. Oxford: Oxford University Press.

Schore, A. N. (2003). Early relational trauma, disorganized attachment, and the development of a predisposition to violence. In M. F. Solomon & D. J. Siegel (Eds.), *Healing trauma: Attachment, mind, body, and brain* (pp. 107–167). New York, NY: Norton.

Schore, A. N. (2005). Attachment, affect regulation, and the developing right brain: Linking developmental neuroscience to pediatrics. *Pediatrics in Review*, 26(6), 204–211.

Schuder, M. R., & Lyons-Ruth, K. (2004). "Hidden trauma" in infancy. Attachment, fearful arousal, and early dysfunction of the stress response system. In J. D. Osofsky (Ed.), *Young children and trauma intervention and treatment* (pp. 69–104). New York, NY: Guilford Press.

Stern, D. (1985). *The interpersonal world of the infant.* New York, NY: Basic Books.

van der Kolk, B. (2014). *The body keeps the score: Brain, mind and body in the healing of trauma.* New York, NY: Penguin Books.

3

Arranging the Environment to Reduce Children's Stress and Support Healing through Play

In this chapter, we discuss how early educators can create healing environments that reinforce messages of safety and calm for children who have experienced trauma. As we discuss below, trauma-responsive environments for young children include a foundation that provides a wide range of opportunities for children to participate in play that supports them to learn new skills, cope with stress, build resilience, and help them rewire their brain and body toward healing.

How a teacher arranges the environment in the classroom is essential to providing a felt sense of safety for a child. It is also important to remember that what helps one child feel safe may not be the same for another. Given this, it is important to individually ensure that every child has a safe person, object, place, or activity they can find that helps their body be calm. Table 3.1 includes examples in the environment that can lead children to feel a sense of safety.

In the next vignette, Director Samantha Watson-Alvarado describes how the use of visual schedules to promote predictability, routine, and safety can help children manage their stress levels when there is an expected or unexpected change in their routine.

DOI: 10.4324/9781003326113-4

TABLE 3.1 Example practices that support children to feel safe

Practice	Examples
Adults who are nurturing and lead children with their presence to feel safe and regulated	Adult uses soft tones of voice (even when child is dysregulated), body language that conveys "I am here for you" vs. "I am coming after you." When a child is dysregulated, the adult does not react harshly but instead pauses and wonders what they can do to help the child feel safe
Reducing visual clutter and disorganized spaces	Reduce the amount of wall covered with artwork Reduce clutter on the teacher's desk Reduce the number of materials provided to children (too many choices = overwhelmed) Reduce classroom clutter
Predictable transitions	Providing children with advanced notice when a transition is coming next Routines and the schedule each day are predictable and children know what is coming next Minimal unexpected changes occur unless advanced notice is provided
The use of visuals to help scaffold what is coming next	Using visual or auditory aids (e.g., timers, visual schedules, chimes) Paired with a verbal cue that a transition is coming
Safe spaces to get away	Comforting locations with comforting activities or objects in the classroom where children can get away (for 1–2 children)
Nature elements	Sand, water, loose parts, nature items
Big body movement	Children have access to play that allows pushing and lifting heavy objects, squeezing, jumping, running, climbing
Child-directed play	Access to free play that is led and directed by children Allowing children to choose the play and activities in which they are interested Adults reduce direction and correction surrounding play
Access to materials that interest the child	Adults pay attention to what interests the children and provide materials with those related themes (e.g., they are fascinated by a rainbow after rain and the teacher provides paint to create a rainbow on paper)

TABLE 3.1 Cont.

Practice	Examples
Soft and soothing colors	• Avoid colors (i.e., red, orange, yellow) that promote arousal • Lighter-colored rooms are perceived as more open, less crowded ("spatially available"), and thus safer and more calming • Natural colors such as beige can evoke outdoor images and promote calm
Activities that calm the stress response system	Mindfulness, breathing, art, water/sand play, movement, music, playing instruments, riding a bike
Objects that help the child feel safe	Blanket, teddy bear, pacifier, picture of a family member
Reducing emotional triggers for individual children	Anticipate triggers of individual children and help them prepare when that event is coming (e.g., warning a transition is coming or a change in the schedule)

"Teacher Abdullah is Safe Doing Grown-Up Work, and We Hope to See Him Tomorrow": How Our Preschool Uses a Visual Schedule to Assure Children that Adults Will Not Disappear—Samantha Watson-Alvarado, Director, Comprehensive Therapeutic Preschool

Just as adults use calendars and to-do lists to remember what is next, children benefit from visual reminders. One therapeutic preschool uses a visual schedule (Figure 3.1) every day to review and explain to the children which adults will be present the next day at school and where any missing adults may be and why.

If a teacher is out sick, the classroom instructional assistant or substitute teacher might say, "Teacher Cynteria is safe at home taking care of her body and we hope to see her tomorrow." Or, if a teacher is absent due to a meeting, the children might be told, "Teacher Abdullah is safe doing grown-up work and we hope to see him tomorrow."

The term *safe* is important in this classroom because the children have all experienced chronic stressors and trauma and a grown-up being absent may be a trauma reminder for a loss,

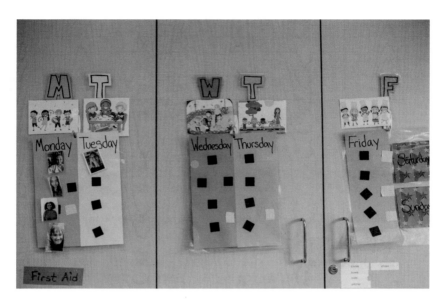

FIGURE 3.1
Days of the week visual schedule.
Source: Comprehensive Therapeutic Preschool.

separation, or abandonment. The term *hope* is also intentional. We use the term hope to prevent children from setting expectations about when they will see their teachers again and then being disappointed if it takes longer than they desire.

Using language with more certainty, "We will see Teacher Eric tomorrow," puts teachers in the position of possibly not being able to hold a promise they make to the children, which can create disappointment, erode trust, and become a potential trigger for children with a history of loss and disrupted attachments. So, we always say, "We *hope* to see Teacher Angeline tomorrow…"

Director Samantha Watson-Alvarado explains how they use the visual calendar in the preschool:

The Days of the Week visual schedule is part of our everyday lunch routine. Making tools like this part of the daily schedule promotes consistent use. The teachers in the comprehensive therapeutic preschool use pictures (visual) and their spoken words (auditory) to talk about the current day and the day to come. Including pictures and having it hang in a place where children can easily see it assists them in remembering; providing them with a tool to continue processing the information after the teacher has already reviewed it. The visual serves as the reminder of what to expect during the current day or the next day. We use the calendar to reassure the children that the grown-ups at the school are safe—a message that can reinforce safety and security. For children with trauma reminders about adults/people who disappear in their lives (e.g., divorce, foster care, incarceration deployment), this communicates consistency and provides children with time to process a change in their routine. For example, if we know a visitor is coming to a classroom needing to do an observation, we will ask for their picture ahead of time so we can explain to the children who is coming to visit us, why they are coming, and to reassure them that this visitor is a safe person.

Reflection/Discussion Questions

◆ Why do you think some children need a visual to serve as a reminder of what to expect and what is coming next during the day?

◆ Can you remember a child who became dysregulated during a transition or maybe when there was an unexpected change in the schedule/routine? How might a visual schedule be used to help that child?

Create a Safe and Calm Area in the Classroom

Children who are impacted by stress in their lives, including trauma, when triggered, will instinctively seek a safe person, a calming place, a comfort object, or regulating activity to help their stress response system to feel safe again. Providing children with a dedicated spot in the classroom is one way that educators support children to find safety. These spaces are called

FIGURE 3.2
Cozy place.
Source: Busy Bee Preschool.

different names depending on the preference of the school or program: calming spaces, relaxation corners, vacation stations, zen zones, just to name a few examples. They are not intended to replace an attuned, empathic adult (Figure 3.2).

Establishing a safe zone in a classroom can have many benefits for trauma-impacted children and can build coping skills for all children as it helps them:

- ◆ Build regulatory resilience (e.g., feeling safe, disrupting reactivity, cultivating a regulatory pause)
- ◆ Develop self-awareness (e.g., identifying sensations in their body, feelings, awareness of thoughts, and the size of their feelings)
- ◆ Recognize when they have big feelings, are feeling scared, and need a break
- ◆ Pause to open the cortex for problem solving, engaging back into the class activity, talking about what happened with an adult, and thinking about the best way to solve an issue for the greater good.

Jenna Ornbaun works with early educators in the San Francisco Unified School District to think about care spaces and how to help children feel safer. She offered this advice on an area that is often overlooked as a potential safe space (Figure 3.3):

> I go into preschools and look at the outside space, and the thought is that "this is where children run." But outside should also be a place your kids can sit and reflect and relax. We can help them by making sure there's shade and quiet spaces. As children, many of us were not given spaces outside that had places for reflection, contemplation, and quiet play. So, try having art outside, or having books outside, so that children can choose those small, contained, safe spaces without having to engage in a way that overwhelms their stress response system.

This classroom has the following in their safe space:

- ◆ A rainbow, sun, and clouds
- ◆ A blue spinner chair to sit in. It can turn around for 360° quick viewing or movement to provide regulation
- ◆ Fluffy brown rug on the floor to sit on, lay down on, or roll yourself up in like a burrito
- ◆ A comfy couch

◆ A brown rocking chair
◆ Pictures of children from the classroom using the safe zone to calm and regulate their bodies.

FIGURE 3.3
Quiet calm space.
Source: Comprehensive Therapeutic Preschool.

This space is available any time of the day and can be used with an adult to support co-regulation or on the child's own (self-regulation). At the beginning of each school year, we teach the children how to use the space and the materials in it. We limit this space to no more than two children at a time.

– Samantha Watson-Alvarado

Safe and calming spaces should never be used as a form of punishment! For trauma-impacted children, the meaning of their stress-related behavior is often, "I feel unsafe." When we react fast with punishment, blame, or consequences, it will decrease their sense of safety and increase their fight, flight, and/or freeze reactions. We can think of safe spaces not as a punishment but as an invitation to calm down. Table 3.2 includes two examples demonstrating this contrast.

When you begin planning for your safe or calming area, here are some key considerations:

- ◆ *Location and colors.* If possible, place the safe zone away from loud, busy, or high-traffic activity areas such as blocks and dramatic play. Ensure a child can see their teachers and that the adults can still supervise the child.
  - Use cool colors (i.e., blue, green, purple) that have a calming effect.
  - Avoid deeply hued warm colors (i.e., red, orange, yellow) that may arouse the nervous system.
  - Lighter-colored rooms are perceived as more open, less crowded ("spatially available"), and thus safer and more calming.
  - Avoid stark white walls.

TABLE 3.2 Examples of punishment vs. safe and co-regulatory responses

Child's behavior	Adult reacts with punishment/consequence/ correction or demand	Adult responds with an invitation to a possible pathway to a safe and co-regulatory place
Hitting other child	"You don't hit your friends. How would you like it if they hit you? You need to go calm down in the safe space"	"You hit him. Your body must feel angry about something right now. Should we take a walk together to cool down or go to the safe zone together?" When the child appears calm and is ready to re-engage, the teacher invites them to have a conversation about what happened and some choices they could have made instead of hitting. The teacher also helps the child make repairs (e.g., apologize, say what made them angry, negotiate a compromise for next time)
Taking another child's toy	"Go to the safe space. I will give you 5 seconds to get there, or I will call your mom"	"You really wanted that toy. I know it is hard when you can't have what you want right away. It can leave us with big feelings. Sometimes if we walk away and take a break it can help. Shall we do it together or do you want to go to the safe space by yourself?" Teacher prompts suggestions of what the child can do with their big feelings when they are in the safe zone (e.g., blow bubbles, draw a picture of their feeling, read a book)

◆ *Materials that promote calm.* The list below gives examples of materials that can support children in regulating their distressed bodies:
   • Music with headphones
   • Sand
   • Playdough
   • Coloring books
   • Crayons/markers/colored pencils/paper
   • Bean bag chair
   • Fidget toys
   • Painting

- Blankets/pillows
- Sand tray/sand toys
- Calming lotion
- Bubbles

◆ *Introducing the safe space in the classroom.* When you introduce new materials into the classroom, it can automat-
ically excite the sensory response system of children
(something new!). They get excited and filled with big
emotions. Or some kids become nervous from the uncertainty of the new object/activity and change in routine.
Knowing that a new item, change in routine, and a new
tool can cause activation of stress (positive and adverse),
it is best to think in advance how to introduce the safe
space to children slowly. Here are some tips:

◆ *Talk about the safe space—what it is for and why children
would use a safe space.* For example, "We all have big
emotions and feel worried or scared. When that happens,
sometimes it can help to find a person like a teacher to
help us but sometimes we just want to be alone and get
away to a safe space to help our body find calm. This is
the safe place in our classroom to get away if your body
tells you that you need a break. You are not alone; your
friends are still around; you can leave at any time and the
teachers are there if you need them. But this is a space for
one child or one child and their teacher if you decide that
would help you. It is not a punishment. We invite you to
use if but only if you think it will help you."

◆ *Practice how to use the safe space when the children are calm.*
When children are calm, circle time can be the best time
to engage them in learning how to use the safe place.
Practice can help them learn the expectations and how to
use the space when they have an emotional emergency.
Following is one way you might practice with children.
Read a book to children during circle time where the
characters have big emotions or a big problem. Have the
children volunteer to pretend to be that character. They
can practice identifying that their body is stressed and
then going to the calm area to select one or two strategies
in the safe space that might calm their body. Making it

fun, engaging, and interactive while practicing can help the children associate positive feelings with the safe space. Then, when they are triggered emotionally in the future, that safe space will evoke positive connections and emotions.

◆ *Expectations and rules that help everyone feel safe.* Simple rules can help everyone feel safe. Rules such as:
  • One child at a time unless the child asks an adult for help
  • An adult can join if the child makes that request
  • An adult can join if the child or others are not safe. It is the adult's job to make sure everyone and everything in our classroom is safe
  • Keep our objects safe and protected
  • An adult will check in with you to see if you want to talk or need help

"The S Stands for Superhero and Safe Space": Building on the Children's Interest to Help Them Find their Safe-Making Superpower!—Shirley Strensfeld, preschool teacher

In this vignette teachers help children use the theme of superheroes to understand that they have two sides of themselves, one that can feel scared and another that can help them feel safe. They use this powerful metaphor of the superhero to help children find their special powers that they can use when they feel worried or scared. The center, in a large urban area of Indianapolis, enrolled children from communities with high cumulative risk factors, including poverty. Most of the children and families experience ongoing stress and trauma, although their specific histories are not always made available to the preschool staff.

Recently, the teachers started to notice that many of the children were using superhero themes in their play. They were pretending to be Spiderman and other superhero figures throughout the day. They were also acting out their stress through behavior such as hitting, swearing, and yelling. In response to these observations, the teachers created a safe place in the classroom for the children. A few months later when the children were familiar with this new space in their classroom, the teachers decided to build on the theme of superheroes and connect it to the class safe place. They introduced a superhero cape: a red cape that had a big S stitched on the back. The teachers explained, *"The S stands for superhero and safe space."* They talked to the children about how everyone has two different parts of themselves when they are scared and/or when they have big emotions. We have our scared self and our safe self, and they reinforced, *both sides help us to stay safe.*

This is how Teacher Shirley described the cape to the children:

> The scared side makes us run away or hurt things or others and sometimes it makes us freeze like a statue. That side is doing its best to make us react fast when we feel big emotions or feel scared, but it does not always keep others or ourselves safe. But we have another superhero side, the safe side, that can help so we don't react fast and hurt others, ourselves, or things around us. This superhero cape can help us find new ways to feel safe. Like finding a safe person, a safe place, a safe object, or a safe activity that can help our body feel calm and regulated again.

Teacher Shirley explained this strategy, along with the cape, helped the children see there is a side of all of us that gets scared or has big feelings, but we all have another side, a superhero, who can come in and help us find a safe place, person, or activity that can help our own bodies feel safe.

Reflection/Discussion Question

◆ Can you think of ways that you have helped children acknowledge their fear or worries but at the same time helped them recognize another side of themselves that has the power to protect them and help them feel safe again?

"Two Sides of Ourselves": Why This is Important in Play

When children are triggered over and over from their traumatic stress, they may begin to internalize a message, "I am always bad" or "The world is a scary and unsafe place." One way to help a child disrupt that internalized narrative that develops from ongoing stress is to help them see there are many parts of them that can be accessible at the same time. For example, "This is my worry brain talking and then I have another side that can tell my worry brain that we don't need you now—instead I need my calm brain to help me find a solution." It can be helpful to name each part: "I call my worry brain Maurice and my calm brain Star." Then a teacher can say, "How can we ask Star to come and help us this moment feel safe and calm?"

The idea of the cape can help a child access a bigger, stronger, wiser part that helps them solve problems for the greater good, think and reason, feel safe, and access strategies to calm their big emotions. It is important that we don't label their parts good or bad. Instead, we say that all of our parts are here to help but when we are worried or scared, we do have one part that is always available to help us be healthy and strong and not hurt others, ourselves, or things around us.

Environment Strategies that Calm the Sensory Response System

Each child has a unique sensory system. When a child is triggered emotionally or their perceived safety is threatened, they move out of the optimal zone of arousal into hypo-aroused (freeze––the sensory system slows down) or hyper-aroused (flight/fight—the sensory system revs up). The strongest pathway to regulate that child is the relationship with an adult caregiver

TABLE 3.3 Environment strategies that can calm children's activated stress response systems

Auditory	Tactile	Natural outdoor environments
Eliminate low-frequency sounds	Pat or rub the child's back	Nature
Hum or sing	Provide textured blankets	Animals
Increase calm or soft voices to support relaxation	Crumple paper	Sand
	Water or sensory table	Fountains
	Playdough	Water
Play instrumental music	Art projects	Photos of nature
Play white noise	Sand	Plants
Play nature sounds	Fidget toys	Trees
Go to quiet area	Give self-massage	Loose parts
Go to noisy area	Animals	Play outside
Listen to music	Textured stuffed animal/objects	
Headphones with music choices	Vibrating toys	
	Squishy balls	

Vestibular	Visual	Olfactory
Rock	Dim the lights	(many children are sensitive to smells so we must be careful)
Swing	Reduce clutter on walls	
Bounce	Safe places	
Sway	Safe objects or bins	Smelling lotions
Ride in a stroller	Safe person	Scented stamps
Take a walk with an adult	Visual schedules/cues	Smelling jars
	Label toys/areas	Fresh outdoor air
Movement	Transition cues	Flowers
Run	Clearly defined areas	Cotton buds dipped in a scent
Ride toys	Timers	
Shake	Nature	Scented erasers
Dance	Animals	Scented stickers
		Scented playdough
		Scented balls

Oral	Proprioceptive	Other ideas?
Take a drink	Jump, climb, run, walk	
Chew on a toy	Yoga	
Eat food	Blanket burrito	
Take deep breaths	Push heavy toys	
Suck or bite on lips	Trampoline	
Pacifier	Stress balls	
Eat a popsicle	Squeeze objects	
Talk about feelings	Push hands on wall	
	Weighted balls	
	Squeeze hugs	

with whom they feel safe. There are other pathways in the environment that can also help a child regulate their body.

Table 3.3 lists several environment strategies that can calm a child's activated stress response system. These are general recommendations to consider and it is important to recognize that what is calming for one child may not be for another. For example, one child may be regulated by music whereas for another it may give them energy or even dysregulation. From Table 3.3, can you identify what you are already providing for children as well as any strategies you could add or strengthen in your early learning environment?

Creating Boundaries and Reinforcing Safety with the Use of Trays

Inviting children to use trays during their play is one way to create physical containment and safety within the environment. The example below shows a tray that provides a contained space for each child with limited boundaries to work within. This contained space that only one child can work in can give the child a personal place to feel safe, where they can create within an area that belongs to them and that they do not have to share with others. Additionally, Figure 3.4 shows tape dividing each area so that children know the width of the space they can work in. Within their work space, every child is making moon sand (an easy-to-make sensory experience using flour and oil). The sensation of the moon sand in their hands can be an additional tactile environment activity that promotes regulation for most children. If a child is sensitive to the texture of the sticky moon sand, the sand can be placed in a Ziploc bag and the child can squeeze and mold it without the sand getting on their hands.

Trays can:

♦ Provide a more contained environment and support a child to be less overwhelmed and during clean up

FIGURE 3.4
Reinforcing safety through trays.
Source: Comprehensive Therapeutic Preschool.

◆ Promote a quieter environment, helping to lessen the stimulation of the activity. When a child is less worried about having to share materials and space with peers, they are more able to focus and concentrate on their own play

◆ Adaptations for children who have sensory sensitivities, by placing the moon sand in a Ziploc bag.

Moon Sand: 1/4 cup baby oil to every 2 cups of flour. Mix together. If it's too sticky, add more flour as needed.

"Having This One Little Thing, That Was So Very Small, Is What she Needed": Creating Safety Through Kinetic Sand: Valentina Torres, mental health specialist

Simple materials can help children promote regulation to feel safe. In this vignette, Valentina Torres describes how she worked with a young girl who found safety through kinetic sand.

> One little girl, Marta, I was working with was attending a school site where someone had recently driven their car right into the classroom. The driver was drunk; he crashed his car into the classroom during school hours right at pick-up time. After he crashed into the building, he got out of the car and started to run through the classroom. The children and teachers were so frightened of him that they ran to hide in the bathroom and other places. Marta had to hide in the closet with her mom and some of her teachers and other classmates.
>
> When I started to work with her shortly after this incident, she was very, very fearful. I noticed that certain play materials like kinetic sand, which is cool to the touch, were very helpful for her. She also loved to play with small sensory water beads which are also cool to the touch. There was something about small sensory materials and something about the coolness of the temperature that was just enough to help her to calm and to participate in play. Being able to first pick at it and then to start slowly to put a whole finger in and then her whole hand was helpful for her. She had a very intense experience when the car crashed into her school, a physical full-body experience. Having these opportunities with these very small materials that she could 100% control is what she needed. Eventually this led into her love of playing with playdough. She would smash it down. That was one of the ways she got out some of the energy charge in her body.

This young child was able to find regulation through sensory play and in particular kinetic sand. Because Marta was in charge of how she played with the materials it also gave her agency, choice, and control.

Access and Opportunities to Participate in Different Types of Play

It is important that children have access to a wide range of play and play materials. Every child is unique and will have individual preferences, interests, and materials that they prefer. We could not possibly provide a comprehensive description of all the play activities or materials that should be included in high-quality early learning programs, but we highlight some of the essential materials and types of play that support trauma-impacted children to reduce their stress and to build coping skills when dysregulated.

Children need a daily schedule that includes large chunks of time for play—at least one solid hour in the morning and another hour in the afternoon. Children really need time to get into their play. If we want children to develop their attention span (and the therapeutic benefits… reduce stress, build resilience, heal…), which are desired outcomes of preschool, it is important to plan for long periods of play. They are less likely to experience the benefits of play when it is broken into smaller chunks of time—20 minutes here and 30 minutes there.

(Barb O'Neil)

Sensory play. Children who have experienced trauma may be too scared to explore, discover, and take risks. They do not feel safe and they are too frightened because their brains tell them that their survival depends upon maintaining a hypervigilant state and constantly scanning their environment for danger (e.g., tracking the adult to prevent their own abandonment, competing with other children for toys and materials). *This makes it very diffi-cult for them to play.*

> For children to engage in play, they must trust that their primary caregivers will keep them safe and ensure that their basic needs—including food, water, and protection—are met.
>
> When children are preoccupied with their own sur-vival, they are prevented from using cognitive energy to imagine new and interesting possibilities for their toys and play materials or entering into imaginary play frames that depart from the world right in front of them (what they perceive).
>
> (Nicholson, Ufoegbune, Maniates, Williams, Yee, & Erazo-Chavez, 2022)

When children use their cognitive energy to maintain a sur-vival state, they will have less capability to use their imagin-ation, experiment, explore, and make discoveries with materials through play. As children begin to feel safe, they will be able to play in creative ways, but many children need other options that allow them to participate in the classroom even when their stress response systems are activated and, ideally, to use materials that can calm their nervous systems. *Sensory play creates opportunities for inclusion and is an excellent way to calm children's central nervous system.*

What are examples of sensory play? Water play, sand play, playdough, goop, sensory mats (silicon or wooden), soft mod-eling foam and clay.

Playdough. When children are hypervigilant and scan the room for danger (e.g., will my teacher leave? will a stranger enter? will the food be available at snack time? will they take my toy, who will be there when I wake up from nap?), they can still engage in sensory play in the classroom—pouring water between cups, placing their hands in the sand, pounding and squishing the playdough. These forms of play offer them access into play without requiring too much cognitively or socially.

These materials do not require peer contact, communication, participation in an imaginary scenario, or the cognitive energy required to engage in problem solving (e.g., how to build a tower with blocks).

Sometimes educators add materials to the playdough to soothe and calm the sensory system. Claire Lock of Nature Play SA describes a recipe she uses for lavender playdough. She explains, "Lavender playdough is as calming as it is engaging. The natural colours and fragrance captivate the senses" (https://natureplaysa.org.au/lavender-playdough-by-claire-lock/).

Play with structured materials. Play with structured materials can support children to build mastery, which is often an experience that is interrupted for children with trauma histories. As with sensory play, providing opportunities for children to play with structured materials gives them access to play when they are stressed and hypervigilant without requiring the full engagement of their cortex. Essentially, structured materials can provide children with a brain break and a chance to regulate before they engage in activities that require more cognitive, social-emotional, and physical energy from them. Examples of structured materials include simple puzzles, pegboards, sorter toys, linking toys, and beads with strings.

Loose Parts Play

Classrooms that include loose parts help children, especially those impacted by trauma, experiment with their own ideas, creativity, and mastery over the environment around them.

Loose parts are "found objects and materials that children can move, manipulate, control, and change while they play...Children can carry, combine, redesign, line up, take apart, and put loose parts back together in almost endless ways...children can turn them into whatever they desire: a stone can become a character in a story; an acorn can become an ingredient in an imaginary soup" (Daly & Beloglovsky, 2014, p. 3).

Examples of Loose Parts

- ◆ Rope, wool, ribbon
- ◆ Funnels, water, buckets
- ◆ Wood (sticks, stumps, boards, coins, branches, wood chips, cinnamon sticks, pegs, beads)
- ◆ Shells, leaves, pine cones
- ◆ Plastic bottles and tops
- ◆ Seeds (acorns, nuts, dried beans, seed pods)
- ◆ Flowers, petals, corks
- ◆ Sand, stone
- ◆ Dirt (mud, sand, clay)
- ◆ Grasses (hay, straw)
- ◆ Textiles (hemp, cotton, wool, felt, silk)
- ◆ Newspaper, cardboard, paper tubes
- ◆ Wooden blocks.

Young children can use loose parts to explore, experiment, and make discoveries about their lives and the world around them (e.g., about their identities, their relationships and opportunities for action) in ways that are challenging or too frightening to explore outside of play. Open-ended materials like loose parts create opportunities for children to organize their life experiences and tell stories about their internal worlds. Loose parts give children a place to bring their life stories. In addition to their therapeutic value, loose parts invite conversations and interactions, and encourage collaboration, cooperation, creativity, and innovation.

Repetitive somatosensory play. Repetitive somato- (i.e., movement) sensory (sight/sound/touch etc.) activities stimulate the brain's core regulatory networks and help children calm their stress response systems when dysregulated (Perry, 2020). In fact, these activities are the fastest way to regulate a dysregulated child (or adult!) as they directly reach the parts of our brain responsible for calming and regulation.

Examples of repetitive somatosensory activities that children should have access to every day and throughout the day include:

- Rocking chair
- Walking or running
- Riding a bike or tricycle
- Jumping (e.g., on a trampoline or in place)
- Climbing (e.g., on a play structure)
- Listening to music, dancing, singing, chanting, or humming (including with headphones on)
- Taking deep breaths, doing breathing exercises
- Stretching, yoga, tai chi, or qi gong
- Drumming and rhythmic use of musical instruments
- Swings, hammocks
- Blowing bubbles
- Breathing activities (e.g., smell the flower, blow out the candle)
- Snapping fingers or clapping hands rhythmically.

FIGURE 3.5
Tire swing.
Source: Julie Kurtz.

The tire swing, through swaying and rocking, supports children's vestibular systems (motion, head position, and spatial orientation) and modulates and calms them (Figure 3.5)

FIGURE 3.6
Climbing structure and seesaw.
Source: Julie Kurtz.

The climbing structure supports both big body movement and proprioception (deep pressure into the joints and muscles) that support calming of the stress response system (Figure 3.6). Additionally, the seesaw supports the vestibular system by stimulating the inner vestibules of the ear which also supports regulation

When a child is triggered, the part of their brain that is activated is the hindbrain/survival brain. This part of the brain, when in fight, flight, freeze, requires activities that are somatosensory to regulate. Therefore, talking, thinking things through, and using words are not the fastest ways to support a child to regulate. Somatosensory activities can act fast to support children to stay within or come back to their optimal zone of arousal.

Big Body Play

Rolling, running, climbing, chasing, pushing, banging, tagging, falling, tumbling, rough-and-tumble, [being] rowdy, roughhousing, horseplay, play-fighting. These are just some of the names that adults give to the boisterous, large motor, very physical activity that young children naturally seem to crave. All are forms of big body play—a play style that gives children the opportunities they need for optimum development across all domains from physical to cognitive and language to social and emotional.

(Carlson, 2011, p. 5)

Children need opportunities every day to be physically active and engage in big body play. Why? Children who live with high levels of stress need opportunities to engage in large motor activities that allow them to release the additional energy in their bodies that results from the activation of stress chemicals.

Not only are these opportunities supportive of children's physical development, but they also reduce the chances of long-lasting impact resulting from the stress chemicals released after their stress response systems are activated. Big body play is a fast and direct way of regulating stress for children and adults so children can have access to their cortex which is necessary for them to learn. High-quality classrooms will guide children to have opportunities to move their bodies all throughout the day…this keeps them regulated and engaged as learners.

I think that big body play is really lacking in early childhood places. Yoga balls, tunnels to crawl through, places where they can roll around, objects to jump off of…we know so much more about the interplay between the body and trauma and the way that trauma is stored in the body. Fidget toys are great, but *our body wants to fidget as well*...in my ideal world, every classroom would have an outdoor space and an indoor space where children could move their bodies. This would create a sense of safety where they can be that big part of themselves.

(Valentina Torres, mental health specialist)

"The majority (89%) of a typical day for preschool children is spent in sedentary activities like sitting or squatting, followed by light activity (8%). In contrast, 'vigorous' activity accounts for only (3%) of a day" (Wood, Essien, & Blevins, 2017, p. 45). The largest rate of expulsion of any grade is preschool. Children need big body movement in order to regulate their nervous systems.

Reflection/Discussion Question

Can you make a list of somatosensory activities that you provide for children? What big body movement do you provide to support children to maintain their zone of optimal regulation?

Dramatic play. When working with preschool-aged children it can be hard to know when dramatic play stops and starts. They seem to exist in a work where the boundaries of reality blur and magical thinking takes their play to fantastical spaces. When adults are willing to watch and listen, a child's storytelling and enactment of their thoughts through play can give them valuable clues into how a child thinks and feels about a theme in their life. Listen closely and you might discover that small parts of a story may be imaginary. Watch and see if the child is trying out a new role in their life related to power, agency, autonomy, or control, or just finding a new voice they haven't used before. For children experiencing significant stress, dramatic or imaginary play may be a way for them to briefly escape a harsh reality. For these children it is especially important for caregivers to tune in and be aware of the potentially strong emotions the child might experience; the adult may need to help the child to take a break. Representing their own life experiences in imaginary play may prove to be too overwhelming and frightening.

Expressive arts: children's 100 languages (Edwards, Gandini, & Forman, 2011). Preschool teachers can design curricula that provide opportunities for children to express their thoughts, feelings, fears, wonderings, and theories about how the world works in many different ways. Examples of these languages include playing, painting, working with clay, drawing, poetry, music, singing, movement, building, sculpting, songwriting, and many other forms of artistic and creative expression.

Expressive arts are a powerful form of expression for young children. Art can help children to identify, understand, and express their own feelings. When children are given the opportunity to do art, they are able to express themselves non-verbally (what I feel inside might be expressed on the canvas of the paper). Additionally, art can give children a feeling of agency, voice, and control over their own world (I get to choose what I create and how I use the materials provided).

Research shows that children who engage in art at school have more empathy and increased emotional literacy (Kay & Wolfe, 2017).

It's helpful to think about art materials across a continuum when thinking about what to offer children. The materials continuum moves from fluid (fingerpaint, shaving cream) to more rigid (pencil, wood) with various items in between like markers, sidewalk chalk, modeling clay, and playdough. Looking at materials on this continuum can help preschool teachers pick out activities that support children. For example, if a young child has been dysregulated most of the day, giving the child fingerpaint may escalate their behavior due to the uncontained, messy, and open-ended nature of the material being used.

Whereas coloring with markers on a piece of paper offers more control and containment.

(Jessica Adler, licensed marriage and family therapist and registered art therapist from Boston, Massachusetts)

The Red is All Over: Listening, Wondering, and "Just Being There"

Samantha Watson-Alvarado, Director of the Comprehensive Therapeutic Preschool, shares the following story about 4-year-old Felix who was hospitalized due to being underweight (he was later diagnosed as "failure to thrive").

Felix returned to school after a 2-week hospital stay where he underwent several medical exams that included frequent blood draws. During choice time, he expressed his desire to do art. I remember him staring off and seeming

FIGURE 3.7
"The red is all over."
Source: Comprehensive Therapeutic Preschool.

unsure of what to do. I sat close to him and acknowledged what he had been through, shared how I had been thinking about him, and invited him to do art any way he wanted. He was quiet for a while then asked for Band-Aids, red paint, and paper. I grabbed the materials and watched him intently complete one step at a time: first the red paint, then the Band-Aids. I sat next to him and made comments like, "The red is all over (Figure 3.7)." "I wonder what's happening here." He asked for help unwrapping the Band-Aids one at a time. As he did this, he shared his story about being poked with needles and seeing all his own blood and how he felt scared. After he put on all the Band-Aids, he lifted his shirt to show me where he still had a bandage. He then requested to keep his artwork up high where no one could touch it or see it. He transitioned into another activity and while he continued to have moments of withdrawal and sadness throughout the day, he was able to seek adult support and accept the strategies we suggested to him. I believe giving him that space to do art was an opportunity for him to express his experience and to test if his teachers could hold what he needed to release.

Early on in my teaching career, I would have been uncertain about how to approach this situation. I may have even tried to redirect it or shy away from it, saying something like, "Blood is scary. Blood is in your body. Painting about it might scare other children." But with this young boy I invited him to release his experience by my *listening, wondering, and just being there*. I wasn't quite sure I knew where it was going or even if I was prepared to hold his story, but his ability to be calm and regulated followed by transitioning to a new activity indicated that it was the right thing to do.

Outdoor play—nature play. Outdoor/nature play is essential for the healthy development of all children and especially important for young children impacted by toxic stress and trauma. Outdoor/

nature play supports children to develop a wide range of skills and dispositions, including attention and short-term memory, creativity and imagination, social competence and relationships (between children and their peers as well as children and adults), physical capacities and pro-nature / pro-environmental attitudes and behaviors (PEER Associates, Powers, & Ren, 2018; Ulset, Vitaro, Brendgen, Bekkhus, & Borge, 2017).

> A study on preschool children from multiple U.S. states concluded that abundant natural materials and outdoor play space reduced competition and conflicts among children and encouraged generosity toward others.
>
> (Dennis, Wells, & Bishop, 2014; PEER Associates, Powers, & Ren, 2018, p. 5)

Outdoor/nature play also has many benefits specific to children's mental health, including stress reduction and replenishing executive attention systems (Atchley, Strayer, & Atchley, 2012). Further, children with access to green space have been documented to have fewer emotional and mental health challenges (hyperactivity, peer conflicts, risk of mental health disorders) and greater emotional resilience (Balseviciene et al., 2014; Flouri, Midouhas, & Joshi, 2014; PEER Associates, Powers, & Ren, 2018, p. 5).

In the story below, we learn how Lisa Katzman supports children to regulate, to expel excess energy through outdoor big body movement, and to promote social skills.

"Bob and the Ball": Trauma-Responsive Practice During Outdoor Play—Lisa Katzman, Board-certified clinical specialist in pediatric physical therapy, early intervention and infant development specialist

Lisa Katzman is a trauma-responsive developmental consultant who works to support children with disabilities attending preschool programs. She collaborates with their teachers to create strategies that will strengthen the students' abilities to self-regulate and learn in the preschool classroom environment. Lisa coached Teacher Jason how to support a young preschool child, Bob, through outdoor play.

Bob is a 4-year-old child in the preschool classroom. He lives in a family where there is domestic verbal abuse between his caregivers. Bob is experiencing significant toxic stress in his home. He has been in the classroom 6 months, and this is the first time he is interacting socially with other children.

In his play outdoors, Bob has difficulty with social interactions. When outdoors, he spends the majority of his time throwing balls at other children. He aims at a child and throws forcefully at them, focusing primarily on smaller or younger children. He has not yet shown developmentally appropriate play with others.

The goal was to support Bob in his outdoor play with other children. The teachers wanted to help Bob feel safe and begin to help him learn ways to build friendship skills and to play with other children outdoors. Lisa works with Teacher Jason who works in the classroom with Bob. Teacher Jason found several strategies to help Bob and the other children to stay safe.

Strategies Teacher Jason Used to Help Bob and the Other Children to Feel Safe Outside

♦ Use a gentle tone when talking with Bob.
♦ Choose words such as, "Our classroom is a safe space. My job is to keep you safe and other children safe. When you throw balls at others it hurts their bodies. Let's think of ways to throw the ball that are safe."
♦ Inviting him to discover other ways that he can throw the ball that won't hurt others. Teacher Jason might say, "We could throw the ball at the wall, throw it at the fence, or make sure we throw it to another person if they give permission and we are playing catch." Or he could say, "Bob, can you think of a place where could we throw the ball safely?"
♦ Noticing that Bob likes big body movement, lifting heavy objects, and active kinesthetic play, the teachers provide Bob with more opportunities to climb, jump, push, lift, and throw objects so that he has an opportunity to play

FIGURE 3.8
Pushing a heavy sleigh outdoors.
Source: Los Medanos College Child Lab.

in a way that is regulating to his stress response system. Figure 3.8 shows an example of Bob pushing the heavy metal sleigh outdoors. Bob loved pushing this object and it provided him with the regulatory and proprioceptive input (deep pressure into the joints; see textbox below) that he needed to help his body feel calm.

Proprioceptive play: Big body movement and input through deep pressure to the joints and muscles to support regulation.

Many children outdoors took turns pushing the weighted sleigh shown in Figure 3.8 around the outdoor play structure. The deep pressure into the joints of their muscles (called proporioceptive) and big body movement were regulatory activities for many of the children.

FIGURE 3.9
Pushing a canoe and tires.
Source: Peter Pan School, Alameda, California.

Figure 3.9 shows an outdoor canoe children push all over the outdoor play yard. They also take those heavy tires in the background and flip them, lift them, and push them. This is another example of big body movement that supports children in expelling energy and moving their body to promote regulation.

What is Proprioception and What Does It Have to Do with Children's Play?

Proprioception is:

> the sense that tells the body where it is in space. It's very important to the brain, as it plays a large role in self-regulation, coordination, posture, body awareness, the ability to focus and speech. Proprioception is the sense that lets us know where our different body parts are, how they move and how much strength our muscles need to use. We receive proprioceptive input from our sensory receptors located in our skin, muscles and joints...Proprioceptive activities can either be muscle work activities or activities that apply pressure to the muscle and joints. Heavy work activities involve pushing, pulling, carrying heavy objects and weight-bearing, such as carrying a pile of heavy books or doing a wheelbarrow walk. An example of a deep pressure activity would be giving your child a tight hug or your child hugging themselves into a tight ball. These activities can provide children with a strategy to be calm, focused and ready to participate.
>
> (https://occupationaltherapy.com.au/proprioception/)

Examples of Proprioceptive Activities

◆ Jumping, climbing, running, and walking
◆ Yoga
◆ Blanket burrito
◆ Pushing or lifting heavy toys/objects
◆ Trampoline
◆ Stress balls/weighted balls
◆ Squeeze toys/objects
◆ Pushing hands on the wall
◆ Squeeze hugs
◆ Playing instruments

Strategies the Teacher Used to Guide Bob from Aggressive to Cooperative Play with Other Children

The goals for Bob were to teach him listening, turn taking, and noticing cues from other children. They did that using the following strategies in outdoor play.

- ◆ Back-and-forth throwing of the ball with a teacher. "I throw and you catch the ball. You throw and I catch the ball."
- ◆ Practice soft, medium, and hard throws. The teacher would add the practice of slow and soft throws, medium-speed throwing, and faster and harder throws back and forth.
- ◆ The teacher offered short, predictable time periods for him to practice and tolerate building a new skill. The short and predictable time helped him increase his tolerance for this new task over time. They practiced setting a timer for 1 minute and taking turns. Bob's job was to ask the teacher, "Do you want me to throw soft, medium, or hard?" Bob listened to what the other person needed and delivered that, and the teacher would do the same with Bob.
- ◆ The teacher invited other children to join Bob's game. He practiced listening, taking turns, and noticing the cues from other children. The teacher scaffolded the play with positive connection by saying, "You are taking turns; you are listening to how the other child likes to play."

Lisa explains, what worked for Bob was learning what he needed in play to help his body feel safe, regulated, and calm or to co-regulate him back to the optimal zone of arousal. Proprioceptive and deep pressure activities really helped Bob, and we named the method "Bob's Big Body Play." We built pathways into the environment that would allow him to lift, push, pull, and throw things that were safe. Instead of saying no, we said yes!

References

Atchley, R. A., Strayer, D. L., & Atchley, P. (2012). Creativity in the wild: Improving creative reasoning through immersion in natural settings. *PloS One, 7*(12), e51474.

Balseviciene, B., Sinkariova, L., Grazuleviciene, R., Andrusaityte, S., Uzdanaviciute, I., Dedele, A., & Nieuwenhuijsen, M. (2014). Impact of residential greenness on preschool children's emotional and behavioral problems. *International Journal of Environmental Research and Public Health, 11*(7), 6757–6770.

Carlson, F. M. (2011). *Big body play: Why boisterous, vigorous, and very physical play is essential to children's development and learning.* Washington, DC: National Association for the Education of Young Children.

Daly, L., & Beloglovsky, M. (2014). *Loose parts: Inspiring play in young children.* St. Paul, MN: Redleaf Press.

Dennis, S. F., Jr., Wells, A., & Bishop, C. (2014). A post-occupancy study of nature-based outdoor classrooms in early childhood education. *Children, Youth and Environments, 24*(2), 35.

Edwards, C., Gandini, L., & Forman, G. (Eds.). (2011). *The hundred languages of children: The Reggio Emilia experience in transformation* (3rd ed.). Santa Barbara, CA: Praeger.

Flouri, E., Midouhas, E., & Joshi, H. (2014). The role of urban neighbourhood green space in children's emotional and behavioural resilience. *Journal of Environmental Psychology, 40*, 179–186.

Kay, L., & Wolfe, D. (2017). Artful coalitions: Challenging adverse adolescent experiences. *Art Education, 70*(5), 26–33. https://doi.org/10.1080/00043125.2017.1335542

Nicholson, J., Ufoegbune, V., Maniates, H., Williams, T., Yee, S., & Erazo-Chavez, R. (2022). *Principals as early learning leaders: Effectively supporting our youngest learners.* New York, NY: Teachers College Press.

PEER Associates, Powers, A. L., & Ren, Q. (2018). *Literature review: Nature-based play and learning.* Retrieved from PEERassociates.net

Perry, B. (2020). *Understanding regulation.* NN COVID Series 5. Retrieved from https://youtu.be/L3qIYGwmHYY

Ulset, V., Vitaro, F., Brendgen, M., Bekkhus, M., & Borge, A. I. H. (2017). Time spent outdoors during preschool: Links with children's cognitive and behavioral development. *Journal of Environmental Psychology, 52*, 69–80.

Wood, J. L., Essien, I., & Blevins, D. (2017). Black males in kindergarten: The effect of social skills on close and conflictual relationships with teachers. *Journal of African American Males in Education, 8*(2), 30–50.

4

Play-Based Instructional Strategies that Support Children to Cope, Build Resilience, and Heal from Toxic Stress and Trauma

This chapter provides a deep dive into authentic vignettes and descriptions of instructional strategies and ways to organize the early learning environment to support children to engage in therapeutic forms of play.

A Play-Powered Approach

Barb O'Neil, the Founder and Executive Director of Transform Challenging Behavior, coined the phrase *"play-powered approach"* to emphasize the central role of play in the care and education of young children. A play-powered approach uses playful interactions throughout every aspect of the day in early learning programs—to strengthen relationships, integrated

DOI: 10.4324/9781003326113-5

into curriculum and instruction, to support skill building, ease transitions, and to reduce stress and build children's ability to cope with difficult situations.

Central to a play-powered approach is learning to *accept children's offers.*

Early childhood educators who take a play-powered approach aim to accept the offers children communicate inside and outside of play. This strategy, drawing from theater improvisation, is rooted in goals of supporting human connection, collaboration, and healthy human development across the lifespan (Lobman, 2003, 2018). The key idea is that anything anyone says or does is *an offer* and our goal in communication is to build on these offers. Imagine two actors doing improvisation on stage. One says, "I'm so hot in here." That's an offer. If the other actor responds by saying, "Actually, I'm freezing," they are not building on, but instead, *negatIng the initial offer*. We don't want to do this with children. Instead, we want to look for children's offers—what they communicate to us verbally, non-verbally, and through play—and instead of negating them, we need to ask ourselves, *"How can I say yes-and? How can I accept and build on this child's offer?"* When we use this "yes-and" approach, we are better able to *build relationships and trust* with children. Barb O'Neil explains:

> I discovered that with children who are limit testing— for example, a child who walks into a room and kicks things for seemingly no reason—it's very easy for us to have a knee-jerk "no-but" reaction, which is dismissing that child's offer. I'm not saying we should let children do whatever they want, but if we can train ourselves to observe the child, always asking ourselves the question, *"What can I say yes to?"* instead of responding with a "no-but" or reminding them of the rule, this allows me to build a positive relationship with the child. If I make a practice of looking for the things to say "yes" to, then, when there are times that I do need to remind children of a rule or redirect them, they are more likely to listen because we have built trust and rapport together.

"Annalee Doesn't Listen, So I Looked for Offers to Say Yes"

The teacher in this vignette, Barb O'Neil, uses an approach she calls, "yes-and" with a young child named Annalee. Her approach was to accept the child's "offer" in play and then follow her lead, giving the child a new-found voice and agency in the relationship.

Annalee was 4 years old and lived with her grandmother who had a lot of life challenges. I met her when I was working as a floating special ed teacher. Everyone in the program kept telling me the same thing: *Annalee doesn't listen.* No matter what kind of question I asked about her—What are the goals for her learning and development? What is a typical day like for her? What are her strengths?—the only response was some version of, "You know, Annalee really doesn't listen." It was clear to me that the adults in her life were feeling challenged by her.

I was, honestly, a little intimidated to work with her. Yet, I was determined to use my concept of *looking for offers and saying yes-and* to connect with and build my relationship with her. When I first met her she was doing what we call limit testing. If the cots were out, she would walk on them. If somebody told her to do something, she would either say cocky, cocky, cocky, or just walk away. What I discovered by observing Annalee was that she really loved to go play in the housekeeping or dramatic play area. And so I used that as an opportunity to join her and see if I could follow her lead and play with her. I tried to use a mirroring strategy. So if she picked up a baby doll, I would pick up a baby doll. I tried to do the same activity or a complementary one, so if she was cooking, I would sit at the table and say, "I'm so hungry," or something like that.

One time when I tried to stand up and go get something, she turned around and she said, *"You no move."* I was not expecting that. I'm thinking to myself, "How do I say yes-and?" I reminded myself we were not transitioning, or cleaning up, we were not in the bathroom, I was not leading circle time. *We were playing.* So, I allowed her to be in control of the script and she continued to tell me versions of "Stay there. Be quiet. Don't move." After this game went on for a while, it finally hit me. I was in "time out" and she was reversing the roles that she typically experienced—giving herself the voice and agency to put me, the adult, in time out, a position she was all too familiar with outside of the play frame. My approach was just to accept her "offer" in play and follow her lead. I knew that she and her family were really struggling and I believed it was really important to give her this space to be on the other side of the time-out experience. It was an opportunity for her to be that in a powerful role and have some agency.

Over time, Annalee was really growing to trust me. With our relationship beginning to blossom, I focused my attention on helping her to develop relationships with her peers. I knew that Fiona would be open to a friendship with Annalee so I began to look for offers each of them made that I could use to connect them. If I heard Fiona saying, "I'm cooking spaghetti," I would say, "Oh, go tell Annalee you're cooking spaghetti!" and I would do the same in reverse. As the two children started interacting with each other more and more, if I had an errand to run or we had to go down the hall to the bathroom, I would pair them together to encourage their friendship to develop. I saw Annalee's play skills really develop with Fiona; in particular, they especially loved to pretend to cook together.

A few months later, the entire class was watching a movie and Annalee did not want to join the group. She was in the kitchen and the lead teacher was trying to decide whether or not to allow her to remain there or to require her to come to sit with the class. I suggested, "Maybe just allow Annalee to remain over there; she's not causing any disruption." And, then next thing you know, *Annalee gathered some teacups and she brought them over to the movie watchers*. Pretending to be a server, she made sure that the entire class had either some plastic food or a beverage to enjoy while they were watching their movie.

It was in moments like this that I observed Annalee had developed this emerging new skill of connecting with her peers through play. We started by supporting Annalee to scaffold friendship skills by first learning to play with an adult where she felt most safe and it was easier for her and less overwhelming than playing with peers. Learning to feel safe by playing with one adult successfully was an important first foundational step that later led to learning how to play with one friend and/or several peers.

Reflection/Discussion Questions

♦ Have you ever helped a child build a new skill by learning what is of interest to them (offers to say yes) and introducing a new skill you want to teach within the context of their interest (e.g., with a child who loves to pretend cook in the dramatic play area, this is where you teach them about emotions by placing the feeling chart)?

♦ Can you describe a time you worked with a child and had to scaffold into small measurable steps a plan to help them learn a new skill? Can you describe the steps you took to slowly help that child build a new skill?

Establishing a Relationship First is Important for Children to Feel Safe to Play

Lafeshia Edwards, mental health specialist, reminds us that the foundation of all curriculum and instruction in early learning programs is building attuned and trusting relationships. It is only when children feel a sense of safety and belonging in the classroom that they will be able to play:

In the beginning of establishing a relationship with the child, it is absolutely essential to play in safe ways that the child is initiating and open to engage in. Building rapport, trust, and safety take time and familiarity when children are creating new relationships with unfamiliar people. Developmentally appropriate play is a great way to build trusting connections. Once trust and safety are established, moving into the therapeutic process of using play as a healing agent can begin.

Play-Based Learning across a Continuum

Play-based learning is an approach to curriculum and instruction in the preschool classroom that emphasizes the use of play to support children's learning across all domains of their development. Teachers carefully plan for play *and* they allow for flexibility and invite children's spontaneous play and emergent interests and discoveries (Rendon & Gronlund, 2017).

It is helpful to think about children's play as representing different points along a continuum (Figure 4.1; California Department of Education (CDE), 2021; Jensen et al., 2019; Nicholson, Ufoegbune, Maniates, Williams, Yee, & Erazo-Chavez, 2022; Zosh, Hirsh-Pasek, Golinkoff, & Dore, 2017). In high-quality early childhood classrooms, teachers plan for children to participate in a variety of different types of play across this continuum, including:

- ◆ *Child self-determined play* (sometimes called "free play") is a foundation of young children's healthy learning and development (CDE, 2021). Play is centered on the dynamic and emergent capacities, skills, and interests of the children. Children are given agency to choose their activities and materials, ask their own questions, define and solve their own problems, and explore and make their own discoveries through both solitary and collaborative experiences.
- ◆ *Adult–child collaborative play.* To maximize learning, teachers also provide guided-play experiences. Adult–child collaborative play, or guided play, allows teachers to focus children's play around specific learning goals. Children initiate and direct their play based on their

FIGURE 4.1
Play-based learning across a continuum.
Source: Hannah Shack.

interests and internal motivation. Adults build on the children's ideas and interests to expand and extend the play in ways that support the development or strengthening of certain skills or knowledge.

◆ *Adult-planned and directed play.* Motivation for play emerges from adults' interests and goals for children's learning. Adults prepare environments and materials and plan and implement activities to provide children with practice in specific concepts, skills, and dispositions. The role of the child is to follow along with adult directions, but they should be actively engaged during the activity.

Children need many opportunities to engage in self-determined and adult–child collaborative play. *For most children birth–kindergarten, adult-planned and directed play should be limited.* The balance among these different types of play will vary across programs, based on an approach that is responsive to the child's developmental level, interests, and cultural backgrounds, and is aligned to the goals of the families and the philosophy of the early childhood program or school.

It is important to recognize that some children with trauma histories may prefer more structured play as open-ended activities can be stressful for children who thrive best in environments with high levels of predictability and consistent routines. Other trauma-impacted children might do better with free play where they can make choices.

Trauma-Sensitive Morning Drop Offs

Drop off at preschool can be very stressful for a child. When children are allowed a few minutes between drop off and the start of the day to play on their own or with peers, depending on their choice, research shows that they have reduced levels of stress behaviorally and biologically.

Lynneth Solis, researcher and lecturer,
Harvard Graduate School of Education
(*Source*: Center on the Developing Child, 2022)

Play-Powered Transitions

Transitions can activate the stress response system as children are required to mobilize energy in order to move their bodies from one activity to the next. For most children that activation during transitions is minimal (e.g., volume 1 or 2 out of 10). For trauma-exposed children, that mobilization sends an already activated stress response system to be triggered even more than the other children in the classroom (e.g., volume 9 or 10). Barb O'Neil states, "that early childhood programs—even very academic ones—can be *playful during transitions* (Table 4.1). One way to diminish the stress is to make transitions playful and fun. Most experienced early childhood teachers do this already—playful teaching is part of the folk culture of early childhood—but it has become a bit lost over the years."

"Let's Pretend We're Bulldozers"—Barb O'Neil, Founder, Transform Challenging Behavior

> What I'm talking about is, instead of just announcing clean-up time, encouraging the children to be playful, "Let's pretend we are bulldozers" or "There is lava on the floor, and we have to be really careful about how we walk to the library to make sure the lava does not touch us...." The same playful approach can be used at circle time and/or for large-group activities...singing directions rather than just saying them, having the children imitate gestures or clapping, using finger plays...making a teacher-directed experience really interactive and engaging and playful. Being play-powered in these ways will not only engage children but also prevent a lot of challenges in their behavior from emerging.
>
> (Barb O'Neil)

TABLE 4.1 Play-powered transitions

Instead of...	Try...
Announcing "Clean-up time"	Inviting children to be vacuum cleaners, to turn on their motors and vacuum until the room is cleaner than it has ever been…
Saying, "Mateo, you need to clean up, it is clean-up time"	Saying, "Mateo, let's be butterflies and caterpillars. Do you want to move slowly like a caterpillar toward each object to clean up or fly to them like a butterfly?"
Announcing, "Maria, you can't go outdoors until you clean up"	Announcing, "Today we can be elephants and use our long and very strong trunks to clean up. Let's all make a trunk with our arms and suck up all the toys on the ground with our trunk"

Reflection/Discussion Questions

- ◆ What are your ideas for fun and engaging play-powered transitions?
- ◆ How could you shift a transition you often use with young children to be play-powered?

"Mom Will Be Leaving when the Sand Gets to the Bottom on the Hourglass"

Sal Mana, a preschool teacher working at an urban Head Start program, shares a story of how he and his team supported a young preschool child who was finding it stressful to manage drop offs and pick ups with his newly separated parents.

Bobby is a 4-year-old boy in Sal's classroom. Bobby's parents recently split up, so Bobby has two homes now. On Tuesdays and Thursdays he lives with his dad Victor and the rest of the week he lives with his mom Joanna. Sal noticed that since his parents separated, Bobby's behavior has changed. Bobby often gets upset during pick ups, stomps his foot, and refuses to leave because he wants dad to come instead of mom. Other times he wants mom. The transitions are becoming increasingly challenging for him. Bobby has an especially hard time during drop offs with mom. He doesn't want to say goodbye to Joanna, so he cries. When she tries to leave, he tells her he doesn't want to stay at school. Teacher Sal notices that when he cries, Bobby hides his face behind Joanna's body. Sal thoughtfully creates an environment to support Bobby during this difficult transition.

Sal creates a safe space. Sal provides Bobby and his mom Joanna with a quiet space where they can spend time together at the morning drop off before saying goodbye. It is a small room in the classroom with a child-sized table, books, toys, and art materials. Bobby chooses to draw with his mom sitting next to him. While Bobby is drawing, Joanna sets the 10-minute sand timer provided by Teacher Sal. She reminds him that when the sand goes to the bottom of the hourglass, she will be leaving. After a few minutes, she says goodbye to Bobby and Sal steps in the room. They have developed a special goodbye ritual called "The Chicken and Potatoes Goodbye." Since chicken and potatoes is his favorite home-cooked meal that his mom makes, they turned it into a goodbye ritual with the help of Sal. When the 10-minute timer goes off, the ritual begins. First mom pours lots of spices (kisses) all over Sal. Next, the mashed potatoes are lots of mushy hugs. Then, it is time to say goodbye and, by then, Bobby is laughing and smiling. Sal comes nearby to create a warm hand off with a teacher with whom he feels safe and connected.

Transitions can be a vulnerable point for children who are experiencing something stressful. In order to transition and move from one activity to the next, the body has to activate small amounts of stress chemicals (cortisol). This can go unnoticed for most children. But for children who have experienced trauma or recently stressful events, the body experiences that small dose of a stress chemical and the request to move from one thing to the next as a bigger trigger than normal. In the case of Bobby, it may remind him of moving from home to home and this can trigger him into fight, flight, or freeze.

Embracing Stories (Even Scary Ones) Children Bring into The Classroom

Adults don't want to see a child bring scary topics into their classroom. Plus, none of us want children to experience pain. This innate drive to want children to be healthy and happy can cause us as adults to be overwhelmed by the scary topics and to avoid them or to try to cheer the child up so they are not sad. Additionally, teachers may take a stance of "That is silly; you shouldn't be bringing up these kinds of things." It is so important to pause the impulse to make children happy and instead, learn how to embrace the stories they bring and that are a part of their inner world of emotions and lived experiences.

"Jeremy is Scared of Monsters at Bedtime": How He Learns to Deconstruct His Monster to Feel Safe Again

Let's enter into the inner world of Jeremy as we begin to learn about his fears and how he learns to cope.

Jeremy is 5 years old, and his mom told the teachers that he is having difficulty falling asleep at night. Mom reports that Jeremy is scared and cannot fall asleep without her laying with him every night. He wakes up frequently with nightmares about something scary. Jeremy has not been able to tell his mom what he fears or what is in his nightmares.

Jeremy started to draw a visual image of his fear both at home and school. Every time a teacher or his parent asked Jeremy about his drawings, he would start shaking and run away and hide (flight reaction and freeze reaction). Jeremy was using the drawing to communicate his fears because he was unable to use words currently. The drawing was a way for him to communicate his inner world of emotions and fears. He describes his drawing as a two-headed monster with horns, sharp teeth, claws, and a pouch (like a kangaroo) that melts humans to make them easy to eat and digest.

Jeremy's teacher could support him to feel seen and heard and to name his fears without pushing him to tell his story when he is not ready. Pushing Jeremy with too many questions may trigger him out of the optimal zone of regulation. Taking his lead and asking an open-ended question may help him find words to express his fears. It is best to start slowly.

Following are several ways that educators can respond when they see children communicating their fears and worries through art in the classroom:

Listen with no narration or questions.

Some children are in the middle of big emotions and feel worried, scared, or unsafe. They are not yet ready to use words and may never be able to. Another way to help them feel seen and for their feelings to be heard is to sit close by them and convey co-regulatory and attuned relational support. This can be done with a pat on the back, close proximity to the child (that is adjusted based on the child's comfort levels), staying calm and attuned to what the child is drawing, and sometimes a few words, such as, "I see you are drawing something very important. If you would like to share anything about it, I am here when you are ready."

Say what you see. Describe what you observe in the picture without evaluation or commentary.

"I see a monster with two heads with feet hanging out of their mouth." "I see a very large figure with several eyes and claws." Before inserting yourself into a child's play, consider whether an action will lead the child to feel safe and guide them to regulation or if interacting will lead them to the path of dysregulation. The more you get to know a child's individual needs, the better chance you have of learning how much the child can tolerate you entering their play space and making observations. These guidelines are designed to provide attuned support, but only if the child's individual sensory system can tolerate the interaction in the moment. When the child feels safe, entering into their space and being curious about their picture can help many children have that felt sense of "You see me, you notice what I am doing or how I am feeling, and I am valued and important." Noticing without evaluation is like naming what you see as if you were a camera. There is no opinion (i.e., what a pretty picture) or evaluation (i.e., you worked so hard painting that picture), just describing objectively what you observe.

> Simply naming what you see in a child's drawing is one way to communicate that you are attuning to the child and care about who they are and how they feel. It is a way of validating them and their experience. Your engaged and nonjudgmental presence and words reduce a child's stress and calm their activated stress response system.

Say what you see + ask an open-ended question.
Saying what you see is like having a camera and narrating what you observe objectively. Next you can insert an open-ended question to pull for more information. Avoid pushing a child to talk past their level of comfort. When you try to narrate what you see and/or add an open-ended question you can pay attention to how the child responds (are they open or closed to engaging?). If the child responds by engaging, that can be a sign they are ready and feel safe to talk with you. If the child avoids talking or appears to pull away from the conversation with discomfort, this may be a sign they are not yet ready. In this case you can give the child space and come back to talk with them again at a later time or date when they might be ready.

Examples that *combine say what you see + ask an open-ended question* might be:

♦ "I see a monster with two heads with feet hanging out of their mouth [say what you see]. Is it trying to scare someone [ask an open-ended question]?"

♦ "I see a monster with two heads and several eyes [say what you see]. I wonder if it is trying to hurt someone [ask an open-ended question]?"

♦ "The monster looks like it's eating someone [say what you see]. What is the monster trying to do [ask an open-ended question]?"

A teacher in a classroom working with Jeremy might observe him drawing a photo of a scary monster. The teacher might feel worried, and that worry can activate the teacher's stress response system. Sometimes when an adult feels worried or uncertain as to how to respond, they might react in one of these ways with children:

♦ Avoid talking about it and say nothing or walk away.

♦ Tell the child, "Don't draw such frightening things. You might scare your friends. Can't you draw a picture of something nice?"

♦ Redirect the child to play with and/or create something less alarming.

♦ Shame the child by saying, "That is just silly."

♦ Other?

As adults we react in one of the above ways because we feel uncomfortable. When we react with one of these strategies, we miss an opportunity to hear the meaning behind the behavior, the story behind the drawing, or the feeling/fear they are having. A teacher can instead tune into the child and what they are trying to communicate by combining say what you see + ask a curious and open-ended question.

Say what you see + ask an open-ended question + seek a solution, resolution, or powerful ending

Children must have their cortex (executive/thinking brain) open for business (feel safe and regulated) to be presented with this third option, called "seek a solution, resolution, or powerful ending." You can ask yourself the following questions before proceeding with this next addition:

- ◆ Do I have a secure relationship with the child, and does the child feel safe with me?
- ◆ Does the child generally feel safe in my classroom?
- ◆ Is the child in the optimal zone of regulation in the moment when I attempt this third option?
- ◆ Is the child regulated more than dysregulated?

Using this next strategy can help the child find power, control, resolution, or a powerful choice or ending to the emotional story that is being conveyed through their play.

Here are some examples (building on what we practiced earlier):

- ◆ "I see a monster with two heads with feet hanging out of its mouth [say what you see]. Is it trying to scare someone [ask an open-ended question]? Is there anyone that could come in and save the person from being hurt [seek a solution, resolution, or powerful ending]?"
- ◆ "I see a monster with two heads and several eyes [say what you see]. I wonder if it is trying to hurt someone [ask an open-ended question]? Are there any words we can say to the monster that will make him scared and run away [seek a solution, resolution, or powerful ending]?"
- ◆ "The monster looks like it's eating someone [say what you see]. What is the monster trying to do [ask an open-ended question]? Is there anything you can think of that can help the person being hurt by the monster so everyone feels safe again [ask an open-ended question]?"

Using Stories and Books that Promote Resilience

Jeremy's classroom has an assigned mental health consultant who comes in once a week to support the teachers and students in the classroom. Mental health consultant Marika is familiar with Jeremy, and he feels safe with her. Marika sat with Jeremy in the "safe zone" in the classroom while the other children were outside playing. She invited Jeremy to share the picture he drew if he felt comfortable. She asked if he wanted to talk about it. In the beginning he said "no" because "it is too scary." Marika told him he is safe and does not have to talk about it until he feels ready. After a few weeks, Jeremy told Marika that he was ready to tell her about the pictures he had been drawing. Jeremy verbalized that he knew monsters were not real, but he could not help feeling scared.

With his hands visibly shaking and his lips lightly quivering, he told the story of the monster described below:

> Jeremy said that he could not go to sleep because he had a nightmare of a friendly-looking monster who would walk into his room. But once in the room, two heads, fangs, horns, and claws would pop out unexpectedly. The monster would take his mom, dad, and brother and put them in his pouch which had a liquid that would begin to melt his family in the pouch. Then the monster would eat his family while they screamed for help, but Jeremy could not help them. He asked Marika not to tell his mom because he was scared if he told her, it would come true.

The therapist read the book called *Go Away, Big Green Monster!* with Jeremy. This book helps children go on a journey where a monster is built up page by page and then the child has the power to use their imagination to gain power over the monster by deconstructing it one page at a time. It helps the child learn the power of imagination to create a monster but also to make it go away. The reason the therapist read this book with Jeremy is that books can act like a script mirroring the internal worries or fears of a child and provide ways to handle and cope with their fears. When a child hears in a book how a character coped in the same situation, it can act as a pathway to build a coping/resilience strategy.

After reading the book together, Marika invited Jeremy to add to his picture something that might help Jeremy have power over his imaginary monster/fears and to help find something to make it go away. Jeremy added a superhero who would come in to "destroy" the monster if it tried to hurt his family at night. In this way, Marika helped Jeremy use his imagination to gain power over his fears. Shortly after he had created this drawing, Jeremy began to sleep on his own without his mother lying with him and he was able to sleep through the night. Jeremy said it helped to put his picture in a drawer next to his bed because it kept the monster away. The mental health consultant worked with mom and the teachers to communicate this plan so that everyone was on the same page about how to support Jeremy during bedtime.

Biblio-support is the process of reading to children books that are related to something they are experiencing. The book helps them expand their perspective, provides a new way of looking at their problem, or helps find a solution to what they are experiencing. It helps the brain open neural pathways of hopeful possibilities and aids in building coping mechanisms.

Reflection/Discussion Questions

Have you ever had a child who expressed their fears through a drawing?

1. What, if any, were your fears? Did you have one of these adult reactions?
   - Avoid talking about it and say nothing or walk away.
   - Tell the child, "Don't draw such frightening things. You might scare your friends. Can't you draw a picture of something nice?"
   - Redirect the child to play with and/or create something less alarming.
   - Shame them by saying, "That is just silly."
   - Other?

2. Have you tried to narrate (say what you see) or combine a narration with an open-ended inquiry question? How could you help a child seek a solution, find resolution, or a powerful ending?
3. Have you ever used a book to help a child identify feelings and find a healthy solution?

Learning to Take Deep Breaths Throughout the Day

Bessel van der Kolk (2014), internationally renowned expert on trauma, encourages every adult to learn to use their breath to calm their stress response systems when activated. He also encourages teachers to teach this to young children from their earliest years. He explains:

> When we inhale, we stimulate the sympathetic nervous system (SNS) which makes the heart increase (accelerator). Exhaling stimulates the parasympathetic nervous system (PNS), which decreases how fast the heart beats (brakes). In calm individuals, the inhale and exhale are steady and a good heart rate measures well-being.
>
> (van der Kolk, 2014, p. 269)

Teachers can use breathing to calm children and at the same time regulate their own stress response system. Many teachers have heard of "smell the flower and blow out the candle" to help children breathe to calm their nervous system.

The story below is of a child Carina who in her play buries the baby in the sand. She has gone through some big life changes at home, and it is coming out in her play. Let's learn what the teachers do to help Carina by holding a safe space for her "big emotional" themes.

"Lost and Found: The Baby is Buried in the Sand"

Carina, age 4½, comes from a family where both parents work full time and when they are with Carina in the evening and on weekends, they provide her with undivided time and attention. She recently went from being an only child to having her first sibling. Baby Erik was born just over a month ago. Having attended Western Alliance Early Childhood Development Center from the age of 3, her teachers have communicated that Carina is loving, kind, and developmentally reaching all the key milestones. Over the past month, since Erik was born, there have been shifts in Carina's behavior and in her play.

At drop off, she cries when her parent leaves. At school, she wants to sit on the teacher's lap during circle time and has become increasingly clingy, especially with Teacher Maritza. During her play, she appears to repeat the same theme. There are usually two dolls she calls mom and dad, a little girl doll, and a baby. Carina often buries the baby in the sand, or she will hide the baby under a blanket. Sometimes, when she draws, she puts the baby inside a closet. When her teacher asks gently, "Carina, where is the baby?" she responds, "lost and she can't be found!"

The energy Carina is investing in burying, hiding, or losing her new sibling during play represents her fears of being lost in this new family configuration and worries about a loss of the time and attention and routines she previously had with her parents. This new behavior of clinging to adults is her brain and body's best way of coping with her perception of stress or threat.

Avoid the Temptation to Say, "That's Not Nice" or "Why Would You Hurt the Baby?"

Teachers may feel frightened when they see a scary image of a child in play burying or hiding a baby. It can be tempting to say, "That is not nice" or "Why would you hurt the baby?" In contrast, teachers with knowledge of trauma-responsive practices recognize that, for Carina, this play is her way of expressing her feelings of loss, sadness, and her anger that the baby has changed everything in her family.

For Carina, making the baby go away or get lost allows her to have agency and control through play, which contrasts with her feelings of helplessness in real life. In this way, for Carina, her play is a way of resolving her feelings of worry and distress.

Does This Mean That Carina is Mean-Spirited?

No, this is a developmentally appropriate way for children to express their feelings and teachers can play a very important role in listening, learning, and helping children express how they feel and to cope, manage big emotions (grief and sadness), and find a way to move past/through their fears. When children find ways to identify, express, and manage their big feelings, they build coping and resilience. Coping and resilience can buffer traumatic stress and mitigate long-term adverse effects of a stressful or traumatic experience.

It is important that teachers have self-awareness so that when they observe themes in play that are scary, noticing the emotions this can trigger inside of them is very important for becoming trauma-responsive. When we are triggered and not aware of how we are feeling, it may activate the survival/hind part of our brain to react with the child by redirecting or correcting their play to be "nice" (i.e., be happy, play nice, don't do that to the baby). Teachers who have self-awareness can use the trauma-responsive strategy of pausing and, instead of dismissing the child, can instead begin to acknowledge how a child may feel.

Teachers can also help by creating a felt sense of safety for the child through their tone of voice and non-verbal body language, conveying, "I can handle this very big and scary theme you are acting out in your play. I am here to help you feel safe in our classroom, with our teachers and with your big feelings." By doing this the teacher is able to provide the trauma-responsive strategy of safety, attunement, and co-regulatory support for the child.

Teacher Maritza Attunes to Carina Through Curiosity and Use of Open-Ended Questions

An open-ended question can be delivered when we observe the child feels safe with us (calm body cues, open to engage and not in fight, flight, or freeze) and we know that they are ready to listen, think, or engage. Children's cortex must be open when we are using open-ended questions, and this happens when the child is in the optimal zone of arousal. Below, we show how Carina's teacher uses an open-ended question to increase her feelings of safety by wondering if there is a way to help the baby feel safe. It's important to note that not all the questions described below were asked in one play session with Carina. Instead, Teacher Maritza introduced open-ended questions in different moments while observing Carina in play. Her goal is to support Carina to feel safe. As a result, she is continually monitoring that Carina can tolerate the teacher's inquiry question and that an open-ended question will lead Carina to regulation, not move her outside of her window of tolerance.

Teacher:	Where is baby?
Carina:	Lost, and she can't be found.
Teacher:	I wonder how the little girl feels when the baby is lost?
Carina:	She is happy. Look—she is playing with her mom and dad.
Teacher:	Oh, the little girl is happy because she gets to have mom and dad all to herself to play and have fun.
Carina:	[nods yes]
Teacher:	How do mom and dad feel?
Carina:	Fine.
Teacher:	Are they worried about baby?
Carina:	No.

Teacher:	Will baby be able to eat or drink? What if baby is scared and needs a big hug?
Carina:	[remains silent]
Teacher:	[sits in silence observing Carina and waiting]
Teacher:	Could the little girl go bring baby some food and maybe give a hug?
Carina:	OK. [Carina picks up the little girl and pretends that she brings food to the baby and then gives the baby a quick hug before running back to mom and dad.] Baby is OK now.

Using open-ended questions can support children to:

◆ Feel seen and have their feelings acknowledged
◆ Process their confusing and puzzling feelings
◆ Feel a sense of agency and control (the opposite of a traumatic experience that leaves us feeling a loss of control)
◆ Feel safe
◆ Find ways to work through their big emotions and fears and to find solutions.

Through her play, Carina had a way of expressing her grief and sadness that her family configuration had changed and that there is now a new baby to share the attention and her comfortable, predictable routine had changed with the addition of her new sibling. Carina, also through play and over time, began to help the baby, show concern for its well-being, and build an attachment to the baby, and slowly, she learned how to include the baby in her pretend play with the mom and dad.

How Play Supported Carina's Ability to Cope, Build Resilience, and Heal

◆ Play was a powerful pathway for Carina to express how she felt, especially when it is in the presence of a caring and attuned adult who can bear witness to the story the child is telling through play.

- ◆ Carina had a caring teacher who took time to listen and who was curious about the story that Carina told through her play.
- ◆ Carina's teacher recognized the grief and loss that Carina was experiencing and through play helped her to feel safe, express her feelings, regulate her big emotions, and eventually to find ways to include the new baby into her imaginary world of play.
- ◆ Play is a way to calm big emotions so that we begin to have access to the cortex to think of solutions. Carina needed time to express her sadness and, in naming those feelings through play, she was able to move into the zone of optimal arousal where she could begin to find solutions, such as including her sibling in play and developing a positive connection with her new sibling.

Trauma-Responsive Practices Used to Support Carina

- ◆ *Play is developmentally appropriate.* Play is a developmentally appropriate and trauma-responsive pathway for children to express their feelings and teachers can play a very important role in listening, learning, and helping children express how they feel and to cope, manage big emotions, and find a way to move past/through their fear.
- ◆ *Teacher self-awareness to pause instead of react.* A teacher can build self-awareness so that when they observe themes in play that are scary, it may trigger emotions inside of them that may cause them to want to react to a child by redirecting their play or correcting the play to be more comfortable for them (i.e., be happy, play nice, don't do that to baby). Teachers who have the trauma-responsive strategy of self-awareness can pause and, instead of reacting by dismissing the child, acknowledge how a child may feel by allowing them to express themselves in the world of their play.
- ◆ *Providing children with a felt sense of safety through the teacher voice and non-verbal body cues.* The teacher can intentionally provide a felt sense of safety for the child through tone of voice and non-verbal body language

during a child's play, conveying, "I can handle this very big and scary theme you are acting out in your play. I am here to help you feel safe in our classroom, with our teachers and with your big feelings." Helping children feel safe with the teacher is trauma-responsive and can support the child to build a sense of safety and resilience.

◆ *The use of open-ended questions.* Open-ended questions (when children are in the zone of optimal regulation) can help Carina find ways to work through her big emotions and fears and to find solutions.

Reflection/Discussion Questions

◆ Can you think of a time when you observed a child who expressed a theme in play that was scary? What feeling did it evoke for you?
◆ As you look back, would you do anything different with the child after reading this?

Bibliotherapy: Storytelling and Reading Books with the Purpose of Healing

The National Association for the Education of Young Children (NAEYC) defines bibliotherapy as:

a creative arts therapy that involves storytelling and reading specific texts with the purpose of healing. It is used in many contexts in early childhood education but is especially powerful as a tool to teach social and emotional skills. Because these skills are at the core of what children exposed to trauma need to come to terms with what they have experienced, reading and re-creating stories from picture books makes bibliotherapy especially effective…By supplementing your existing book selection with titles that specifically address dealing with trauma and learning to regulate feelings, you can help children work through their emotions emanating from trauma. Other children without a trauma background will no doubt be drawn to having you read these books, too. But for children with a trauma history, they can be a much-needed tool for healing.

(Colker, Erdman, & Winter, 2020, p. 44)

Books are very helpful for young children impacted by life's stressors and trauma. Children can see characters going through some of the same things they are experiencing—which helps them feel less isolated and alone—and they can also learn from the characters how to cope, reduce their stress, build resilience, and feel safety in the company of safe adults and children. Following are several books that can be tremendous resources for early learning programs supporting young trauma-impacted children:

- *A Terrible Thing Happened* (2000) by Margaret M. Holmes
- *After the Fall* (2017) by Dan Santat
- *Breathe Like a Bear* (2017) by Kira Willey
- *Calm-Down Time* by Elizabeth Verdick
- *Go Away, Big Green Monster!* (1992) by Ed Emberley (control/fear)
- *How are You Peeling?* (2004) by Saxton Freymann and Joost Elffers
- *I'm Not Scared, You're Scared* (2022) by Seth Meyers
- *In My Heart: A Book of Feelings* (2014) by Jo Witek
- *Moody Cow Meditates* (2009) by Kerry Lee MacLean
- *No Matter What* (2008) by Debi Gliori
- *Once I Was Very Very Scared* (2017) by Chandra Ghosh Ippen
- *Ruby's Worry* (2018) and *Ruby Finds a Worry* (2020) by Tom Percival
- *Sophie* (1997) by Mem Fox
- *The Color Monster* (2012) by Anna Llenas
- *The Dot* (2003) by Peter H. Reynolds

- ◆ *The Goodbye Book* (2015) by Todd Parr
- ◆ *The Lion Inside* (2016) by Rachel Bright
- ◆ *The Rabbit Listened* (2018) by Cori Doerrfeld.

Medical play and bibliotherapy: exploring the body, illness, hurt, and life. Everyone has a body! Our bodies all work and function in different ways, and something that is universal for everyone is that the body can get hurt, we can get sick, and one day we will die. Young children might know these things and are curious about them. Child life specialists utilize medical play as a way to help children be curious about these topics in safe ways. Rose Tandeta, a child life specialist, shares that, "Medical play is playing with hospital materials so that kids can process experiences or play out any fears or misconceptions they might have." All children experience medical care at different points in their lives, whether a healthy check up, vaccinations, and/or cleaning off a scraped knee.

Jeanie Liang, who has used medical play with hospitalized children for over 14 years, reminds us that,

> It's important not to force any child to engage with medical play; let it be organic at first. A great place to start is to let it be free play, where the child themselves can elect to go up to a table and explore play items on their own terms.

She offers a cardinal rule, *"only play with materials on someone else's body if they invite you."*

There are a number of easy principles you can follow if you're interested in inviting medical play into your care spaces:

- ◆ Utilize inanimate objects, like stuffed animals, dolls, or paper cut-outs. Directing medical play to an inanimate object makes the play safer because the object will not feel hurt if it gets poked or squeezed.
- ◆ Start with generic medical play toys, such as pretend doctor bags or dress-up materials. If there is a lot of interest

> move on to actual items like Band-Aids, stethoscopes, blood pressure cuffs, gauze, and popsicle sticks.
◆ Watch for themes, comfort, and discomfort, and follow up with parents what you observe.

Bibliotherapy, using books about the body or difficult topics such as death and dying, can be a great way to introduce a topic in a soft way. Children familiar with a book section might benefit from having a book added to the bookshelf that they can select themselves. Jeanie Liang offers this advice related to bibliotherapy:

> It's a non-threatening device or tool, because they can relate to the characters in the book depending on what book you select. Also, if you select a book that has non-human characters, for example, or even cartoon human characters, it's not somebody that they know, and they know it's not them. It's not real, so it gives one degree of separation that can let children be a little bit more comfortable relating to the story.

NAEYC (Colker, Erdman, & Winter, 2020) offers suggestions for reading these books with children:

◆ Open up a conversation about the different characters, their experiences, how they feel about what happened to them, and what they did in response.
◆ Reassure the children that the characters' ranges of emotions are normal and OK.
◆ Ask open-ended questions: "How did __ feel when __ happened?" "What could __ do to feel better?" "Who can help __?"
◆ Make sure to explain that the hard thing that happened in the story was not the character's fault. This is important, as young children often feel that they are responsible for the difficult things that happen to them.

Using Puppets in the Early Childhood Classroom to Support Children to Cope with Stress

Patricia Tatum-Wiggins is the mental health and wellness manager overseeing the mental health component for Redlands Christian Migrant Association, a Head Start organization with 70+ child development centers across the state of Florida. Patricia describes how many of her programs use teacher puppets in powerful ways with young children. She explains that the children they are serving are primarily living below the national poverty guidelines and, as she states, many "are coming from super hard places with most having been exposed to trauma or experienced trauma firsthand." As a result, they focus on creating a safe and nurturing environment for the children, which the puppets support. She explains, "I don't know if you've ever seen children with puppets, but you bring out a puppet and they have smiles. It's just an automatic."

Building anticipation. Patricia describes how one classroom introduced the children to their class puppet:

There was one classroom that had added a third teacher, or an "extra set of hands," to support the external behaviors of the children. The teachers had incredible "buy-in" for using a teacher puppet, and were prioritizing teaching social and emotional skills to the children. To introduce the puppet, the teachers built the anticipation of a new friend coming to visit.

On Monday the teachers told the children that they were going to have a friend who would be joining them some time in the next few days and would be with them for the rest of the year. Every day the teachers would use little teasers to build the anticipation of the children. They would make comments such as, "I wonder when our new friend will be here" or "I wonder who our new friend is." When the puppet arrived in the mail, the Center Director brought the puppet to the door. It was all boxed up so the children had to open it. She said, "You got this package. I'm not sure what it is." The children opened the box and discovered a raccoon puppet inside.

She explained that they had chosen to use animal puppets "so that the children would feel safer." Why animals? Because, she explains, "Typically when children have experienced abuse, it's been at the hand of adults. In order to alleviate a triggering response from a human-looking puppet, we use animal puppets."

Building a relationship. To support the children to develop an attachment with the puppet, the teacher invited them to name it. They brainstormed ideas and then took a class vote and decided on "Chester." She also supported them to do some detective work about raccoons: what is their natural habitat? What do they eat? The goal was for the children to learn the natural habitat of raccoons so they could build a home for Chester. Each of the exercises facilitates a natural attachment between the children and Chester. Bonus: the activities can also be tied to learning outcomes for the children and added to lesson plans.

Supporting a child to cope. Patricia explained that the next thing that happened in this classroom was an example of the power of puppets to support children impacted by stress and trauma. One of the children in the class, Tasha, was dropped off by her grandmother one morning. Grandma told the teacher that her daughter, the little girl's mother, had been arrested the night before, taken out of their home in handcuffs, and Tasha had seen this happen and that Tasha had not spoken since seeing her momma leave. Upon hearing this story, her teacher welcomed her but Tasha would not make eye contact or speak with anyone, including her friends. Tasha's teacher was mindful of her during the morning routine, but gave her the space she seemed to need. After the children came in from playing on the playground, the teacher invited everyone to the large group area and she was holding Chester. The raccoon started to ask the children questions ("Who did you play with on the playground? What did you guys do while you were on the playground?"). He called on a few children and then asked Tasha, "How are you feeling today? Tasha took a few seconds and then she responded and shared that she was sad and scared because her mommy had been taken away by the police the night before. What happened next was heartwarming. There was an immediate empathic response from all the children. Some started to pat her leg; others circled around her. One child said, "My daddy was arrested, and you'll be able to talk to [your mommy] soon." Another shared, "My uncle is in jail and I really miss him." The children started to share stories of their internal worlds that had not been shared previously. After this happened, Tasha was able to talk with the children, Chester, and the teacher about what had happened and how she was feeling about it. Patricia explained, "It was just a beautiful little moment in that classroom of bonding and feeling safe and secure and for that little girl to be able to voice what was going on inside of her."

The third teacher was no longer needed. Patricia reports that after a few months of having Chester in the classroom, the teachers no longer needed the extra set of hands. With Chester's support, they were now able to manage and de-escalate children when stressed and to teach them regulation skills. As a result, this classroom no longer needed the third teacher.

Reflection/Discussion Questions

- ◆ Have you ever used puppets with children to help re-enact situations that they could relate to? If you have never used puppets, is this a strategy you might try with children?
- ◆ Would you give each puppet a biography and place to live? How would you introduce the puppets to the children?

The Moment the Crayons were Thrown to the Ground

Teacher Isa had set up an art activity. DeSean, age 4, joined and started to color. He had been waiting his turn to join the activity, as Teacher Isa was leading children in pairs through a multi-step coloring exercise. DeSean did not like Teacher Isa's project and started to scribble frantically and shout, "No. I hate this school. I hate you." Isa calmly provided

DeSean with two choices: "You can take your paper and color with teacher Reni or you can stay here and make the project with me." DeSean broke a crayon, then quickly took his arm and swiped the container holding all the crayons off the table. He ran away and hid under the trampoline. Isa motioned Teacher Reni to come over and switch with her so she could support DeSean. She knew what caused him distress and she wanted to make things right again.

Teacher Isa quietly and calmly approached DeSean as he was hiding under the trampoline. She crouched down and said, "I can see you're upset. I'm going to sit here and wait for you. We can figure this out." DeSean squirmed his body around and grunted in response. Isa then put out her hand and said, "You're safe at school, DeSean. Would you like to hold my hand?" DeSean put his hand out while still hiding his body under the trampoline. Isa held his hand and said, "I'm here to help you. Can we do something to help you feel better or feel safe again?" DeSean scooted out from under the trampoline and curled up next to Isa. He leaned his head on to her chest while continuing to hold her hand (Figure 4.2). DeSean said, "I didn't wanna do that dumb project. I don't like it. I wanted to make my own picture for my mom." Isa listened and said, "I can help you with that. I can tell you really want to make something special for your mom. We need to first clean up, then we can make a picture for mom. I will help you. What color crayons should I pick up? What color do you want to pick up?" DeSean responded by saying, "I want blue. You, orange." DeSean accepted this idea and was able to draw his mom a picture.

Preschool teachers are faced with difficult moments throughout the day, often many times a day. All young children are learning how to recognize, express, and communicate their feelings, needs, and wants. They are not experts in this skill yet, which means situations that we as adults may deem "easy" can really be quite hard for them. It's important for us to critically examine how our disciplinary approach with young children can positively influence or impede their

FIGURE 4.2
Teacher Isa with DeSean and the crayons on the ground.
Source: Comprehensive Therapeutic Preschool.

development. Some may think of responding in a punitive way, such as, "DeSean, you can't color until you pick up those crayons" or "Hey, DeSean, we don't throw crayons at school. Clean those up now or I'm going to call your parent." Others may feel inclined to walk away from this situation. We may also worry that children will be spoiled if we give in or that other children will copy DeSean's behavior. While those feelings and thoughts may emerge in our minds, it's important for us to respond in a manner that draws out the child's ability to think critically about what happened. By doing so, we acknowledge what he actually did, and what he can do next time, versus what we did not want him to do. This shift in response allows the child to learn and build their skills in relation with you rather than you punishing them for not having yet mastered a developmental skill on their own.

In social-emotional curriculum the premise is to teach children new skills. They have not yet learned how to identify and regulate big emotions and, as a teacher, our job is to teach, not to punish. However, with trauma, the primary and most pressing goal is different. The assumption is the thinking and learning brain is not accessible and the child's primary goal is to seek safety and regulation first before they are capable of thinking, listening, or learning a new way to respond. That is why Teacher Isa's first approach was to help the child feel safe with her. Once DeSean felt safe and calm, Teacher Isa could then redirect him to the activity and teach him a new way to respond. For all children, the cortex must be open for business to listen and learn. This happens only after they are calm and regulated. The most powerful pathway for a child to feel safe and regulated is through a connection with a trusted adult.

Giving a Child a Voice by Looking at the Meaning Behind their Behavior

Daniel, a mental health specialist, will help make transparent that when a trauma-impacted child has dysregulated behavior, it is their adapted way to protect themselves from a previous danger. Understanding that, as adults, we can cultivate the empathy and curiosity required to look below the iceberg to the meaning of the behavior.

"Look Below the Iceberg": Helping a Child Gain Connection— Daniel Nieves Rivera, mental health specialist

Daniel Nieves Rivera, a mental health specialist working at a social services organization, provides mental health services to children, teachers, and families. He shares a story about a young child who has experienced trauma that was reflected in her daily interactions at school.

Sara is a 3-year-old child who lives with her mom Maria and attends a preschool at one of the centers that Daniel supports. Maria reveals that a year ago Sara and herself were victims of domestic violence, but she does not share more information than that. What she shares is that Sara is very quiet and withdrawn at home. When Daniel asks the teachers to tell him more about Sara, what she is like, and her strengths, they share that she is angry a lot and throws toys around the room.

Observation. When Daniel enters the classroom for the first time, he immediately notices Sara. Sara is playing by herself in a corner table of the classroom, away from the rest of the children. This solitary/isolated play continues during Daniel's second visit. Not knowing the details of the domestic violence, he is aware of himself as a male and the triggers that could develop, so he observes from close by but does not approach.

Daniel is mindfully creating an opportunity for interaction, but he wants to see how she feels in his presence first. He joins a group of children building blocks close to Sara. Daniel describes this scene: "I was aware and attentive, waiting for her reaction to see what she wanted to express. First, she looked at me and I was already playing with other kids. I got up and approached her only after she made eye contact with me. I started the interaction by introducing myself: 'Hi, my name is Daniel.' Then I initiated conversation about the horse toy she was holding in her hand. I said, 'I see you like farm animals.' I was trying to resonate with her and follow her interest. Sara didn't join the interaction; she was not ready.

The following week when Daniel visits the classroom again all children are outside in the playground and Sara is sliding on the slide. Daniel is interacting with a few children close by but also paying attention to her, modeling, making eye contact, and noticing that she is looking at him and the other children too. Daniel's intention during this encounter is to act as a link and encourage Sara to engage in parallel play with her peers. Then suddenly Sara opens up. She approaches Daniel and says: "I went to the beach with my mom." Daniel understands that Sara is asking to be acknowledged, to be seen, so he uses this window of opportunity to connect and focuses his full attention on her, and what she is telling him. He asks her what she likes about the beach. Sara says: "I like the sand and I like the wind." After that interaction, Sara feels more comfortable to approach and talk to Daniel more frequently. During his next visit Daniel notices that Sara is beginning to respond to other children's attempts at interaction. For example, two children were playing in the sand and asked Sara when she was walking by if she could hand them the shovel by her in the sand. Sara brought over the shovel and said, "I just went to the beach and built a sandcastle with my mom." The other kids asked if she would help them. Sara ran off but this was the beginning of her accepting an invitation to engage socially.

Children who have been harmed by trauma may protect themselves by shutting down and isolating or by fighting to keep others away. This is an adaptive behavior the child has evolved to develop for survival. To keep others at a distance will help the child feel safe. Healing from trauma can come from small steps to engage Sara in a way that feels safe for her. Daniel was trying to engage Sara slowly and in a way that felt safe for her.

Safe space for teacher reflection. After each observation, Daniel opens a discussion about his observations of Sara with the teachers. He talks about how Sara needs positive relational connections that feel safe for her. Daniel notices that when Sara says something or tries to communicate, it is important to listen, make eye contact, and acknowledge her in front of the children, as doing so allows her to be seen.

Daniel also provides a space for the teachers to share their feelings, allowing them to slow down and reflect about their worries, talk about when they feel triggered, and how that may increase their tendency to react and label Sara, not recognizing that she is trying to communicate a need for belonging and her desire to connect. Acknowledgment of the teachers' feelings enables them to pause, access their cortex, and think, listen, and have a deeper conversation about the meaning behind Sara's behavior. Daniel's goal is to create a space for teachers to reflect and develop empathy and guide them so they can *develop the ability to look below the tip of the iceberg* (Sara's reactive behavior) *and see the meaning underneath her behavior* (she is trying to feel safe and gain connection).

Reflection/Discussion Question

◆ Has there been a time in your work with children when you looked below the tip of the iceberg to the meaning underneath the behavior?

References

California Department of Education (CDE) (2021). *The powerful role of play in education: Birth–8.* Early Education and Support Division. Retrieved from www.cde.ca.gov/sp/cd/re/documents/powerfulroleofplay.pdf

Center on the Developing Child (2022). *Building resilience through play.* Brain Architects Podcast (February 22, 2022). Harvard University. Retrieved from https://developingchild.harvard.edu/resources/podcast-resilience-play/

Colker, L., Erdman, S., & Winter, E. (2020). *Trauma and young children: Teaching strategies to support and empower.* Washington, DC: National Association for the Education of Young Children.

Jensen, H., Pyle, A., Zosh, J. M., Ebrahim, H. B., Scherman, A. Z., Reunamo, J., & Hamre, B. K. (2019). *Play facilitation: The science behind the art of engaging young children* (white paper). Denmark: The LEGO Foundation.

Lobman, C. L. (2003). What should we create today? Improvisational teaching in play-based classrooms. *Early Years: An International Journal of Research and Development*, *23*(2), 131–142.

Lobman, C. (2018). Reconnecting learning to development through performance ensembles. In Burgoyne, S. (Ed.), *Creativity in theatre* (pp. 209–220). Cham: Springer.

Nicholson, J., Ufoegbune, V., Maniates, H., Williams, T., Yee, S., & Erazo-Chavez, R. (2022). *Principals as early learning leaders: Effectively supporting our youngest learners.* New York, NY: Teachers College Press.

Rendon, T., & Gronlund, G. (2017). *Saving play: Addressing standards through play-based learning in preschool and kindergarten*. St. Paul, MN: Redleaf Press.

van der Kolk, B. A. (2014). *The body keeps the score: Brain, mind and body in the healing of trauma*. New York, NY: Penguin Books.

Zosh, J. M., Hirsh-Pasek, K., Golinkoff, R. M., & Dore, R. A. (2017). Where learning meets creativity: The promise of guided play. In R. A. Beghetto and B. Sriraman (Eds.). *Creative contradictions in education: Cross disciplinary paradoxes and perspectives*. Denmark: Springer International Publishing.

5

Case Studies of the Power of Play to Support Children's Stress Reduction, Resilience, and Healing

Applying Ideas Throughout the Book to Your Practice

The six case studies in this chapter are real stories from around the country of early childhood educators and specialists implementing trauma-responsive practices with children in their programs. The purpose of the case studies is to support individuals and/or teams to inspire reflection and learn practices to apply the trauma-responsive practices in the programs in which they work. We provide vignettes followed by a summary of the trauma-responsive practices and reflective questions to discuss as you and your team continue on your journey of giving a voice to every child impacted by trauma.

DOI: 10.4324/9781003326113-6

CASE STUDY #1: "Mason is in Heaven": How Adding a Dollhouse to the Sensory Bin Supported a Little Boy to Move from Grief to Friendship

Julie F., an inclusion specialist providing consultation at Colorado Soaring Eagles Preschool

Background

Vincent is a 5-year-old boy with a history of neglect in his family. Vincent's mother, Rona, has a history of drug and alcohol addiction. His father is a truck driver on the road, frequently traveling. When he is home, he enjoys spending time with Vincent, but he is infrequently present at home. His grandma and grandpa have difficulty with physical mobility but watch Vincent when he visits their house. He has the best smile, loves coloring and drawing, and has a very kind heart. He talks fondly about his dad all the time. Sadly, his 3-year-old brother, Mason, wandered out of the home, walked down the street, and drowned in a local pond a year ago. Social Services have been involved monitoring the family's mental health, physical wellness, and safety ever since. Part of the Social Services monitoring has been to support mom in enrolling Vincent into a preschool program full time. He was connected and accepted into our preschool, and I have been working with him all year in collaboration with his preschool teacher, Claudia.

When Vincent entered the program, he was not sure how to play. He had difficulty sitting still long enough to play, listen, or learn. He did a lot of wandering around the classroom with a lack of focus. When he played with objects, he would throw things, kick things, or bash toys together repeatedly. His play with other children was limited to hitting, kicking, and pushing his peers and shooting people with pretend guns. He would also destroy toys in the room or would lay under a table and just kick the tabletop. He was not very verbal and had some formal speech articulation challenges, likely due to neglect. Vincent's teacher, Claudia, quickly noticed his inability to play.

Reducing Vincent's Stress and Building his Ability to Focus Through Play

Teacher Claudia and I teamed together to develop a trauma-responsive support plan which included increasing his sense of safety by reducing his stress and supporting him to build coping skills.

- ◆ *Reducing uncertainty by increasing predictability and safety.* We wanted to increase Vincent's sense of safety by reducing uncertainty, which we addressed by creating a predictable routine in the classroom. Vincent felt safest when everything was predictable and he knew what was coming next (e.g., I do my circle, I do my breakfast, and then Ms. Julie comes to play with me). We made him a little picture schedule because he would always ask the adults to tell him what was coming next. He used it every day. One day he was in circle time and kept getting up to see what was next on the picture schedule (Figure 5.1). He would mumble his way back to circle, repeating "It is snack time next, it is snack time next." Honestly, his regulation increased when he knew what was next, especially visually being able to see it.

- ◆ *Supporting Vincent's language development.* As Vincent would typically respond non-verbally to questions or communicate using only one-word comments/answers, both Teacher Claudia and I spent a lot of time just talking with him. We would narrate what we noticed he was doing (e.g., you are building a tower, you drew a picture of a sun, you have the orange block in your hand) and ask him questions (e.g., Would you like to have a snack now? Can I add a blue block to your tower? Would you like Jeremiah to join you?). This narration provided him with attunement and a sense of connection but also supported Vincent's language development.

- ◆ *Finding opportunities for Vincent to keep his body in motion.* In addition to observing that Vincent found it challenging to sit still, Teacher Claudia discovered that he could swing for a long period of time and that, when he did, this

FIGURE 5.1
Visual schedule.
Source: Julie Kurtz.

movement helped him focus on activities in the classroom. In the classroom they had an inflated sitting ball. Vincent could sit on the ball and bounce or rock back and forth and this really helped him regulate. We noticed he gravitated to it, and we observed that he would listen better when he was rocking, bouncing, and/or moving. We also put a tree swing outside, and he would crawl into the hammock-like swing and sit in it, rocking back and forth.

"The only way to move from these super-high anxiety states to calmer more cognitive states is rhythm," says Bruce Perry, Ph.D. "Patterned, repetitive rhythmic activity: walking, running, dancing, singing, repetitive meditative breathing—you use brain-stem related somato-sensory networks which make your brain accessible to relational (limbic brain) reward and cortical thinking.

(Perry, 2014)

◆ *Providing Vincent with opportunities for agency and control.* Teacher Claudia identified small tasks that Vincent could be successful with that would provide him with opportunities to experience mastery and a sense of agency and control. For example, she invited Vincent to have a special responsibility during circle time. Specifically, he was invited to come up to the visual schedule in front of all the children at circle time and use the pointer stick to help point to the activity they were learning. So, if the class was learning about the day of the week, he would use the stick to point to Tuesday on the visual. If they were discussing the weather for that day, he would use the stick to point to the sun. This gave him a job and opportunities to feel a sense of agency and control.

Vincent's Gun Play

At the beginning of the year, Vincent walked around the classroom and pretending his fingers were guns and he would regularly shoot at the other kids. When he was angry at Teacher Claudia, he would pretend to shoot her. He even closed one of his eyes as if to aim. Teacher Claudia would say to him, "Vincent, there are no guns at school, not even pretend." If he continued to pretend to shoot her, she would tell him, "We don't allow guns at our school because it is our job to keep you and everyone safe."

After a few months, this type of play decreased as Vincent began to build relationships and trust with his caregivers. When Julie asked Vincent why he wanted to shoot people, he said, "To protect mommy" and "To protect people from bad guys." Julie then asked Vincent if

FIGURE 5.2
Cozy cube.
Source: Busy Bee Preschool.

Teacher Claudia was a bad guy and he said, "Yes. Because she won't leave me alone." Julie then talked with Vincent about how he didn't like it when Teacher Claudia said "no" to him and he communicated this feeling by pretending to shoot her.

Julie shared this conversation with Teacher Claudia and this led her to speak with Vincent directly about his feelings. She explained,

> I know you don't like when I say no guns. When you use a pretend gun you are trying to protect those you love. Remember, my job is to keep you and everyone here safe. If you feel worried or scared or unsafe, instead of using a pretend gun, together we can find another way to help you feel safe.

Vincent came up with some ideas of things that would help him feel safe, such as going to a teacher for help (Teacher Claudia), going to the tree swing outside to swing, reading a book, riding the bikes outside, or hiding in the cozy cube. By the last couple of months of school, Vincent stopped pretending to have a gun at school. He used his cozy cube (Figure 5.2) and swing, and frequently would go up to a teacher to ask them to read a book. He learned new ways to cope with his stress.

How Play Supported Vincent's Ability to Cope, Build Resilience, and Heal

- ◆ Thanks to the creation of a safe person and space for play and provision of materials that represented home and family (e.g., figurines, house), Vincent was able to process some of the feelings around the death of his brother Mason through his play.
- ◆ Play gave Vincent a sense of voice, power, and control over his inner world that frequently sent messages to him that he was unsafe, and people were unsafe.

◆ Play allowed his language to develop, to build stronger relational connections, and to feel safe. This, in turn, helped Vincent rewire his brain and body to be in the zone of optimal arousal more frequently, which allowed him to learn new coping skills such as being able to use words to say how he feels as well as to listen to and play with his peers.

◆ Vincent used gun play as a means of gaining control and imagining he was saving his mommy from danger. This was his best attempt at fighting back to protect those he loves from real or perceived danger. Julie and Claudia were eventually able to help direct Vincent to find other ways to feel safe, such as the cozy corner, drawing, and talking with a teacher.

Trauma-Responsive Practices Used to Support Vincent

◆ *Calm and regulated adults.* An adult has the power to lead children to regulation through their own calm state. Facial expressions, tone of voice, and non-verbal body language send a message to the distressed nervous system of a child, "You are safe with me and can borrow some of my calm to calm your own sensory system."

◆ *A visual picture schedule.* When the cortex is not available because the child is preoccupied with their internal stress, they are unable to focus, listen, or follow instructions with simple next steps provided verbally. Adults who pair a visual aid with a verbal direction have an increased chance of helping the child's cortex pay attention to what is coming next. If the child knows what is coming next with the support of a visual, this predictability can promote safety and regulatory support.

◆ *Cozy cube/corner.* Every child and adult needs to get away to somewhere safe when their emotions feel big or scary or unsafe. When a classroom has a place for a child to get away, a place where they can turn down the volume of their internal stress, they can find a pathway to calm.

◆ *Narration to promote language development and a sense of belonging.* Children who have experienced trauma are preoccupied with survival. This can cause delays in relationships and social skills. But the child still has a neurobiological need (limbic brain) for connection, so when a teacher narrates the positive attributes of what they observe the child doing, the child's limbic brain is lit up with messages, "I belong, I am seen, I am included." In turn, this can provide the much-needed relational attunement that buffers the stress response systems.

Reflection/Discussion Questions

♦ Are there any trauma-responsive practices listed in this vignette that you have tried with a child (whether that child had experienced trauma or not)? How did the child respond?

♦ Are there any trauma-responsive practices you want to add to your toolkit in the future?

CASE STUDY #2: Shifting from "Bad Day / Bad Boy" Towards "We are Working On or Towards…": Taking Intentional Actions to Disrupt a Funnel into the Preschool-to-Prison Pipeline

Lafeshia Edwards, early childhood mental health consultant

Lafeshia received a referral for a young African American boy named Jeffrey, 3 years of age, who was reported by his teachers as having disruptive behaviors during nap time and transitions. Lafeshia shares how a collective team collaborating together can disrupt the narrative that Jeffrey was always having a "bad day" or was a "bad boy."

My first classroom observation of Jeffrey took place during circle time. He was one of the children in the classroom who struggled with sitting for any length of time during circle. He frequently would wander away from circle time. The teachers, Ms. Elsy and Mr. Brian, were trying to help him remain in circle by seating him on a four-legged chair. He would shift from the chair to the floor numerous times during circle. When questions were posed to the group, he would get very excited to answer them and bounce up and down while lifting the chair off the carpet and over his head. This would result in Ms. Elsy saying, "You need to calm down," and she would proceed to ignore him while calling upon another student to answer the question. Throughout circle time his name was often called to signal a behavior correction, "Jeffrey, raise your hand"; "Jeffrey, stop picking up the chair and sit down." I noticed that when he was unable to share his thoughts or answers with the group out loud, he would say them in a low voice to himself, yet loud enough for his nearby classmates to hear him.

I also observed that, during nap time, Jeffrey became very dysregulated once the room became dark. He rolled on to the bare floor next to his sleep mat, talked to himself in a loud volume, and refused to rest when Teacher Brian offered his assistance. His eyes were wide open and his mind/body appeared alert. Because of this behavior, the teachers would tell Jeffrey that if he did not take a nap then he would lose making a choice time during free playtime. The teachers both would frequently say, "Now, now, Jeffrey, let's not be a bad boy right now."

When teachers have high stress working with children who are frequently dysregulated, it can be common for them to default to the voice, "What is wrong with you?" and the trajectory of their reactions from this voice becomes punishing, shaming, blaming, threats. This can cause trauma-impacted children to feel unsafe and worsen their behavior. We will see how the teaching team slowly shifts their voice to "What is your behavior communicating?" so that they can help Jeffrey feel included, feel safe, and learn new coping skills.

Shortly after this observation, I met with Jeffrey's mother. She shared that he had been suffering from night terrors every night for a long period of time. Some nights his terrors resulted in him sleep running in his room and often colliding into the walls face first, screaming and crying, and waking his eight siblings in their household. His mother reported that it was very difficult to wake him from these terrors and to keep him safe. Many days he arrived late to school after a bad night with these terrors and it was on these same days that he would struggle during nap time. I learned that this information had not been shared with the teaching team.

We had our first team meeting about Jeffrey which included Teacher Elsy, Teacher Brian, and the program Director, Marsha. They had all developed a poor image of Jeffrey from multiple challenging experiences. The Director shared, "He has no respect for me. Once he threw a box of Lego™ across the room when I entered his space. I don't understand why he would behave that way in the presence of an authority figure." Teacher Elsy suggested Jeffrey's mother did not care enough to get him to school on time and regularly. As I listened to them, I could see that they were overwhelmed and had lost hope in this child and his family, and they shared a felt sense of powerlessness. They were trying to gain control through punishment, blaming, and consequences.

> As adults we were raised with values and beliefs about how children should behave—values such as children being seen and not heard, respecting authority, spare the rod and spoil the child. These values can impact the way we react to children's dysregulated behavior. An example is when Director Marsha said, "He has no respect for me and I don't know why he would behave that way in the presence of an authority figure."

I could literally feel this child slowly on a pathway to the cold steel bars of a prison. This pipeline, like the grim reaper, silently follows black and brown children from an early start. It creeps in through the words used to describe them by teachers, site directors, county and government professionals, as well as the images that portray them on social media, in music, and throughout society which lead to the discriminatory actions they experience on a daily basis, eventually swallowing them whole once they give up on themselves. I was scared for Jeffrey. I felt compassion for the teachers.

I suggested that we have a second meeting but this time including Jeffrey's mother. During this meeting the staff learned about his sleep difficulty and night terrors at home. We worked out a system to communicate daily about Jeffrey's sleep—brief, hand-written notes were exchanged during drop-off and pick-up times about Jeffery's sleep each night and his experiences in the classroom each day. We also came up with a plan around nap time. Teacher Brian suggested that Jeffrey has a lot of energy at nap time and has a hard time calming his body. Brian thought of a few strategies that might help Jeffrey become calm. He said he could sit close to Jeffrey and read a book and tell him, "It is OK not to nap. After I read this book, you can read a book too by yourself if you are not tired. I will sit right by you if you need anything." Second, they gave Jeffrey a flashlight. They wondered if he got scared when it was dark and that if he could hold a flashlight and see then maybe he would not be so scared. We all talked about shifting our language from deficit to strength-based when describing Jeffrey and his behavior. For example, phrases such as "bad day or bad boy" were transformed into "We are working on or towards _____," followed by naming the small successful steps Jeffrey was taking as he made progress towards that goal. For example, "Jeffrey, we are working on feeling safe and calm during nap."

With time, I saw the best turn-around I have ever witnessed in my career. The staff took steps to create an area for Jeffrey to decompress when he was feeling overwhelmed or needed a break. It featured pillows and soft low lighting with his favorite marine life-themed books and materials to engage with when he was inside this space. Additionally, they included and empowered him during circle times by allowing him to sit on the carpet with all the other children and share his thoughts when he raised his hand. The language they used to describe him had changed from punitive to strength-based. I heard teachers using phrases like, "I wonder if Jeffery would like to model for us how we use this toy" (a lot different than what I had previously observed, which sounded more like "Since Jeffery is not able to sit still, I am going to call on someone else to show us how to use these materials"). Jeffrey started to smile in the classroom more and offer a helping hand with his peers and teachers when he noticed they could use it.

As a team we were able to breathe a little easier knowing that our work together encompassed the greatness of giving this child who was experiencing so many risk factors a voice. Because of our collaboration together we were able to disrupt the possibility that Jeffrey would be silently pushed out of his early learning program and, instead, we worked together to identify trauma-responsive ways to support him in his present environment. We also noticed something miraculous. Jeffrey had difficulty with play. He was so preoccupied in the moment with his own stress and survival that he was not able to relax enough to play. The trauma-responsive practices above were implemented in frequent doses each day to create safety and to re-regulate his stress response system to be more frequently in the optimal zone of arousal. Once the teachers started to see Jeffrey relax and regulate, they noticed he began to play more. He wanted to paint and spent hours using his imagination in the dramatic play area, acting out scenes of superheroes and building towers with his friends.

How Play Supported Jeffrey's Ability to Cope, Build Resilience, and Heal

   ◆ To play a child must feel safe in the moment. When a child's play is limited, it may mean they are preoccupied with survival. First, we must help children feel safe and regulated. The more they feel safe, the more their bodies will relax into the optimal zone of arousal.
   ◆ As in this vignette, once a child feels safe, they can begin the job of play. Play can happen when a child feels safe enough in the moment to stop scanning for danger and can relax into the present moment and lose themselves in the make-believe world they create to learn.

Trauma-Responsive Practices Used to Support Jeffrey

◆ *Adults, by slowing down and through reflection, can regulate and then gain perspective.* Sometimes when we are in the middle of our own movie, we can only see our own story line and have limited ability to see all the other views for each person. To gain perspective, we can momentarily become an outsider looking in at how others feel and the meaning behind their behavior. Lafeshia helped the team to slow down, to regulate their stress, and then reflect to gain a bigger-picture perspective of how each person feels, why they are behaving the way they are, and strategies that can be helpful, especially to Jeffrey.

◆ *Support during nap time to promote safety and calm.* During nap time, when everything became still and children's bodies were calming to sleep, the opposite happened to Jeffrey. His nervous system is wired to be on high alert making it difficult for him to relax his stress levels. So, nap time for him was like being on volume 10 when everyone else was on 0–1. Teacher Brian recognized that Jeffrey needed individual support to help calm his body and mind. He also noticed that this was not always possible, so giving him a choice of quiet activities he could do during nap time helped Jeffrey to feel safe. Finally, they made a hypothesis that the dark may trigger him whereas for other children it helped them sleep more readily. Having a flashlight so he could see helped him feel a sense of agency and control and helped with his fears when it was dark so that he could see around him and scan for danger.

◆ *Moving from deficit to strength-based language and narration.* Our brain has evolved to scan for the negative. This evolution is our brain's best attempt to keep us alive. If we could see danger, we could survive longer. But this default mode of scanning for the negative is not helpful in developing the self-esteem of a child. Children such as Jeffrey internalize the words we use about them. To disrupt this deficit language, we can look at the strength of the challenging behavior. As anr example, a child who witnessed domestic violence (e.g., dad hitting mom) and was never able to protect her is now in the classroom and sees a boy take a toy from a girl. He runs after the boy and hits him. This behavior is the child's best attempt to fight and try to protect the girl now when previously he had been unable to do so.

♦ *Family engagement and collaboration.* It is common to pin the blame on the family when we feel powerless. It is the pathway of least resistance. But it can cause harm. When the teachers disrupted that by meeting with the mom and learning about his sleep terrors, they were able to have a deeper understanding of the meaning behind the behavior, empathy for what mom was experiencing, and, more importantly, a collaborative plan in the best interest of Jeffrey.

♦ *Cozy corner.* Children when in distress scan for a person, place, object, or activity to calm their body. When they can't access a safe adult in the moment, they will seek out a place to go to get away. Some children prefer a safe zone over an adult as their preferred way to regulate their body.

♦ *Shifting from black-and-white thinking—"good boy/bad boy and/or good day/bad day"—to understanding the meaning behind the behavior.* Children who experience trauma are not intentionally doing the behavior to disrespect adults, to purposefully push buttons, or because they enjoy it. They really are scared and don't yet have the experience to calm their own distressed bodies. Using language that shames or is critical will continue to build the internal narrative that the child is not worthy of love or help. An adult can disrupts that mindset by shifting to a voice saying, "What do you need? I am here for you and trying to figure out what your puzzling behavior is communicating right now."

Reflection/Discussion Questions

♦ Is there a child, whether past or present, you can bring to mind who pushes your buttons? Notice the narrative you use about this child (e.g., it is the parents' fault, the child is intentionally hurting others, he is a bad boy or she is a bad girl). Can you practice taking a deep breath and shifting the language to "I am the adult and I am bigger, stronger, and wiser and can create a space with me or in our classroom for you to find safety and calm"? How can you look past the behavior and recognize this is the child's best attempt to cope in the moment?

♦ Can you make a list of children with dysregulated behaviors in your classroom? What is the strength of that behavior that they adapted over time to protect themselves or others (e.g., hitting others = trying to gain a toy because they grew up in foster care moving from home to home and always having to leave their toys behind)?

CASE STUDY #3: "Pedro is Part of Our Class": Small Wins are Huge!

Ryan Kurada, kindergarten teacher

Pedro, a student in my kindergarten classroom, had a very difficult early childhood. He was born to a mother who was addicted to drugs and alcohol. He was taken into protective custody and eventually was placed in a foster care home at a very early age. He came to my classroom really struggling to get that sense of belonging. When he joined our classroom, he did not speak. He did not smile. His face was blank with no emotional expression. When you looked at him it was as if he looked past you. He did not want any interaction with adults, children, toys, or music. It was as if he walked around in a shell, every day. He would come in each day with his backpack on and wouldn't take it off but, instead, would go underneath his desk and curl up in a fetal position. He did this every day for the first 6 months of school.

I knew this child was in terror. Crawling under the desk and curling up in a fetal position was him saying, "The entire world is overwhelming, and everything feels unsafe. Hiding is my only way to cope." I knew that it was absolutely essential that I communicated messages of safety to Pedro every day. It was critical that he know I would never give up on him. One day he peeked at me from underneath his desk and I thought, "Well, that is a start and a huge leap toward him feeling safe with me."

Freeze Reaction

Some children who experience trauma activate a survival mechanism called "freeze" to protect themselves in the midst of stress that overwhelms their stress response system every day. When the daily stress is too much (e.g., caregiver absence, abandonment, abuse) and their body does not have a means to cope, they shut down so that their body can find a way to survive. They bring these same coping mechanisms with them to the classroom.

In October, we were having a beginning-of-the-year event called "Field Day"—with many activities outside—and I had prepared a fishing-game activity for our students. I put together wooden dowels with a string at the end and a magnet. The students would use these fishing poles to fish for different floating alphabet letters on the playground. In preparation for this activity, I had placed all the fishing poles on one of the classroom tables—another place that Pedro liked to hide under. Just as we were about to go outside to play, I noticed that all of the fishing poles were mingled together. At first, I was a bit upset, but then I started to laugh and said, "Pedro, what happened to the fishing poles?" He looked up at me without any expression and did not answer. Even so I thought to myself, "OK, I have an 'in' with Pedro." He is starting to interact by peeking his head out at me to look at what I was doing.

The Meaning Behind the Behavior

It is so easy to jump quickly to assume that a child is intentionally trying to ruin our day or to cause harm. It takes a big trauma-responsive muscle for the teacher to pause and look past the surface of a child's behavior to see the meaning underneath. In the case of trauma, in most instances the meaning behind the behavior is to communicate, "I feel unsafe in the world." For Pedro, peeking out to look may have been a way of gaining Teacher Ryan's attention. Pedro may be saying, "See me, connect with me, and I am starting to feel safe with you."

Then, one day while a group of children were playing together and attaching cardboard tubes together to see how high they could make their sculpture, Pedro came out from under the table and handed the group another tube so it could go a little bit higher. They had such a positive response that he handed them another one. He went back underneath the table but then came out and handed them another tube. And he repeated this over and over until one of the kids called his name: "Pedro, come here and look!" And Pedro started to smile and slowly build trust to join this small group of peers in their play.

Small Wins are Huge!

Most don't realize that these small steps can be what healing trauma looks like. Pedro took a big risk to crawl out from under the table to hand the other children a tube. For him to crawl under the table was *huge*…it was one small win toward healing. It means, "I am beginning to feel safe here and with all of you." Healing trauma does not happen from one strategy or even a few. It is usually small wins. That is, tiny doses of consistency and predictability over time result in rewiring the brain and body of a child to feel safe.

In the spring of that year, we began studying the new "Smart Train" that's running in our community. And we decided to create our own train out of cardboard for the classroom. During a conversation with the class, I asked, "What should we name our train?" And it was Pedro who came up with the idea of what to name it. He raised his hand and said, "What about the 'Epic Smart Train'?" He got to a point where he actually joined us on the carpet. He built up a sense of safety over time where he came out from hiding and joined us on the carpet during circle time. He was still very quiet, but he was with us, and the class appreciated that he was with us, and they communicated this to him every day in many different ways: "Pedro, you are a part of our class."

Trauma-Responsive Practices Used to Support Pedro

♦ *Individualized relational connection.* Sometimes we think that when a child is in distress we should run over to them and give a hug and provide as much love as we can. However, being trauma-responsive is reading the individual cues of a child and saying to ourself:

- *How much close proximity (space between teacher and child) can this child tolerate and still feel safe?*
- *How much voice pitch, tone, prosody, volume can the child tolerate to stay in the optimal zone of arousal?*

A child in freeze does not mean they don't want to engage. Their trauma brain is saying, "Stay away because I feel unsafe" but their limbic brain is saying, "I want connection, I need you to see me." When we recognize both things are happening for a child then we can slowly approach them and trust that in time they will slowly feel safe with us.

♦ *Trauma-related dysregulated behavior is communicating a story.* We repeat this theme as it is an important conceptual underpinning to trauma-responsive work. When we recognize that trauma-related behavior is the child's way of communicating they feel unsafe, then we can depersonalize our adult reaction (e.g., threats, bribes, shame, consequences) and instead say to ourself, "This child's regulatory system has experienced something that has caused him to hide for protection. I will not give up and I can approach the child slowly in a way that sends a message, 'you are safe with me.' "

◆ *It takes small wins to unfreeze and feel safe.* Trauma healing does not come from trying one strategy learned in a book or in training. It comes from implementing one or more strategies consistently in regular doses over time. It looks like small wins, not big changes overnight. It looks like Pedro who feels safe enough with Teacher Ryan, so he peeks out from under the desk to make eye contact as an invitation for engagement.

Teacher Ryan's Advice

In this vignette Teacher Ryan recognized that behavior is communication, and he understood that Pedro was hiding because he was scared and hurting and people and environments felt unsafe. Teacher Ryan suggests:

◆ *Lean on the expertise of a team.* We need multiple perspectives on the child to be listening to that child, to be observing that child: what's working? What's not working? What's a trigger? What's a point of healing for that child? Who can I lean on for support with this child?' Maybe it's not you as the classroom teacher who provides support. Maybe it's someone else like the principal or school counselor.

◆ *Regulate your emotions.* There's nothing we can do with a child if we are at such a point of frustration that we're not able to think clearly. Yes, we're all human and we get frustrated. But we have to learn to take a step back and take a deep breath and acknowledge our emotions and then regulate them. It's challenging work.

◆ *Incorporate diverse types of play in your classroom.* Do you have art? Do you have music? Do you have drawing? Do you have nature? A lot of kids connect to being outdoors as their way to cope and be their authentic selves. As teachers we need to recognize the full range of play opportunities we are offering for kids. If I didn't incorporate constructive play in my classroom, Pedro wouldn't have had an outlet. We need to recognize the power of play and what that does for kids—the different avenues of play are so important for teachers of young children who have been impacted by toxic stress.

Reflection/Discussion Questions

◆ It takes time to build the trauma-responsive practices that allow us to look at children like Pedro with a trauma-informed lens. Have you ever used the following trauma-responsive practices when working with a child?

  • Staying calm and regulated in the midst of a dysregulated child's behavior

  • Looking past the challenging behavior to the "meaning behind the behavior" (e.g., I feel unsafe, I am trying to gain connection, I am trying to avoid too much stimulus)

  • Learning a child's triggers and preventing them from happening in the future by eliminating the trigger, or preparing a child before the trigger happened

  • Identifying a child's strength or passion in play and using that to help scaffold them to feel safe with you or in the environment

  • Leaned on the expertise of others or sought out other perspectives

  • Incorporated diverse pathways of play into the classroom.

◆ Listening to the themes in this vignette, did you learn anything new? Are there any concrete new tools you can add to your toolkit? If not, is there a trauma-responsive strategy you currently practice that you can strengthen?

CASE STUDY #4: "I Don't Want to Leave My Best Friend!" Helping Children in Times of Uncertainty and Stress

Sal Mana, preschool teacher
Sal Mana has been a preschool teacher for 14 years and is currently working at an urban Head Start program in Northern California.

In this case study, Teacher Sal shares a story of how he and his team supported a child who was experiencing a stressful event.

A 4-year-old child named Enna is having a difficult time at home and at school because her family decided to move to a new home, which is very stressful for her. Enna does not want to leave her home and, as a result of the stress she is facing, her behavior has changed in the classroom.

> Stress or trauma is defined by the individual sensory system, not the event. Some children may not experience a move as stressful. But for Enna, her sensory system defined this event as one that is stressful and sad for her. Research shows that the following four factors can significantly increase people's feelings of stress:
>
> 1. Novelty
> 2. Unpredictability
> 3. Not having a voice or choice
> 4. Isolation and feelings of loneliness.
>
> For Enna, a new home, unpredictable new routines, and not having a choice about moving are three elements that are contributing to her compounding stress which is coming out in her behavior and through her play.

During drop offs, Enna is angry and says she does not want to go to school. At home, she constantly expresses that she does not want to move because she loves her old bedroom and home and wants to be close to her neighbor, Mia, who is also her best friend. When Enna comes to school, she picks out dolls and puppets or uses her fingers to create scenes where she pretends to be both the parent and the child. She talks to the figures. This is typically how the scene goes:

Child: I don't want to go over there to that house.
Parent: No, you've got to pack your bags and we have to move.

Child: Sure, OK, I'm ready to do it. But I am feeling really sad, and I don't want to leave.

Parent (yelling): No, we're leaving here!

This type of play and behavior occurs every day with Enna. As her teacher, Sal came up with a strategy to support her. He wanted to make sure to acknowledge Enna's emotions and talk about the changes that are coming for her. Because he knew that when children perceive that they don't have a voice, choice, agency, or control, the situation feels much more stressful. So, Sal wanted to support Enna, through play, to have a voice and opportunity to communicate about the stress she was feeling. Following is an excerpt of one of their conversations together:

Teacher Sal: Enna, it looks like you might be feeling sad. Are you sad?

Enna: [nods head yes]

Teacher Sal: It is OK to be sad. If you want to talk about what is making you feel sad, I am here to listen.

Enna: I am sad because I did not want to move. I will miss my friend who lives near me.

Teacher Sal: You feel sad because you have to move, and you will miss your friend who lives by you?

Enna: [nods yes]

Teacher Sal: Sometimes when we have to say goodbye to things we love or make a big change it can make us feel scared, worried, or sad. What will you miss about your friend and your home?

Enna: I like to play with her. She comes over to my house every day and we climb the tree to our fort, and I will miss that. I don't think I will see her again.

Teacher Sal: Moving to a new home doesn't mean you are losing your best friend. It may mean you have to find a different way to see her. Have you talked to your mom about how you feel? Maybe we could talk to her to see if we can find a way for you to see your friend after you move. Would it help to talk to your mom about how you feel sad and miss your friend?

Enna: [shrugs shoulders] My mom is too busy with the move.

Teacher Sal: Let's think some more about talking to mom but only when you are ready. Would you like to make a gift now that you can give to Mia to tell her how special your friendship is?

Enna: Yes. I'd like that!

Sal then invited Enna to draw pictures for Mia. Together, they planned to create a book that includes Enna's favorite memories that she will give to Mia. Every day when Enna came to school, she sat down and worked on the book. Once Enna started to work on this project, morning drop offs became a lot easier for her. The book became a long project that engaged her for 2 full weeks. It was full of pictures of Enna and Mia playing together. She worked with Sal to express her feelings and her thoughts in the book. Sometimes Sal took dictation, writing down her story ("Mia, you are my best friend because I like to play with you. My favorite thing is when we go to the park and ride bikes together"). Sal also helped her to write a special promise that she wanted to say to her friend, a secret message she planned to share only with Mia. Sometimes Enna did her own writing and she added letters to represent her thoughts and feelings on her drawings. For example, Enna wrote the words "love," "best friend," and "playing" next to her pictures.

Sal decided to read a book about moving to the entire class. The book, titled *Evelyn del Rey is Moving Away* by Meg Medina, describes not only the feelings of sadness and loss that children have when they move but also their resilience and the many positive aspects of moving, including providing families with a new start and new opportunities. Enna seemed to resonate with the story in the book. She listened attentively and after circle time she took the book she was making for Mia and added new details to her drawings and a few new pages. For example, she added the words, "Don't be sad, we can still be friends" to one of the drawings. She added a new picture showing both friends playing together at her new house and building a different fort in the backyard tree.

Giving Enna a place to communicate her feelings in a storybook gift for her friend was a pathway for Enna to process her feelings and to communicate them in a healthy way. As she did this, Sal observed that at drop off Enna's behavior was much better within the second week. One day during pick up she said she was done with the book for Mia. She was very excited when she saw her parent come to pick her up and said, "Mom, can I give this book to my friend Mia? She is going to be so happy." Enna's mother smiled and said, "Of course we can, Mia's mom just called to ask if you wanted to come over for a playdate Friday. Would you like to give it to her then?" Enna's parents showed excitement while turning the pages of her book. Mom looked through the book and said, "This is a beautiful book, Enna. It's filled with lots of good memories you shared with Mia. I think that Mia will be very happy to have this book."

After the book was done, Enna's play evolved to something new. Sal saw her pick up one of the classroom puppets and act out baking an entire meal at her new home. Her play was now *all about cooking and cupcakes*!

How Play Supported Enna's Ability to Cope, Build Resilience, and Heal

◆ When we all have big feelings, we need a place to expel them. When we hold them inside, they can adversely impact our behavior. One way to release big feelings with young children is through play. Acting out the scenes of how we feel through play, especially in the presence of a caring adult, can help a child feel seen and heard and release some of the pent-up feeling they are experiencing in their body.

◆ Another practice was providing Enna with agency and control through her play. When Teacher Sal suggested she make a book for her best friend, it helped Enna express her feelings but, more importantly, to have a way to feel she could control something when she felt out of control from all the uncertainty and unpredictability she was experiencing. Using creative art to express her feelings also helped to regulate Enna.

Trauma-Responsive Practices to Support Enna

◆ *Agency and control.* When children experience uncertainty and stress, their young stress response systems have not yet developed enough coping skills to pull from to cope in healthy ways. They can feel scared and worried, and we can help them by giving them something that provides a perceived sense of having a voice or control over something. When Enna could create a gift book for her friend, it was the very thing that helped her feel that, when her world was falling apart, at least she had control over one thing.

◆ *Giving voice to big feelings through verbal and non-verbal strategies.* Sometimes children have not developed the language, or they cannot find the words, to express all their big feelings. When adults help them find a way to communicate verbally (talking if they can) or non-verbally (acting out with puppets or through play), then this act of projecting/communicating how they feel non-verbally through play can help them regulate their overwhelmed nervous system.

◆ *Story books with themes that children are experiencing.* When a child experiences something stressful and they read a book with characters experiencing the same things, it can help them feel less isolated and alone in how they feel. When the characters in the story overcome their big feelings by using strategies that can support them to feel regulated and safe, then children can imagine feelings of hope and ways to cope.

Reflection/Discussion Questions

◆ Can you think of a child you helped to find non-verbal pathways through their play to communicate their experience to you?

◆ Have you ever worked with a child where you provided them with something that could help them feel a personal sense of control, as with Enna in the vignette above?

CASE STUDY #5: Jerome and His Military Helmet: How My Helmet Protects and Makes Me Feel Safe

Rose Messina, licensed clinical social worker and program manager at a children's hospital

A 3-year-old named Jerome was attending the preschool called Bishop Ranch Head Start. Mental health consultation was provided at the site Jerome attended. He would enter the classroom most mornings in such an intense manner, where he would push teachers, scream at other children, and damage things around him. Drop off in the morning was when he was most dysregulated. The teachers were overwhelmed and would say to the mental health consultant in an exasperated tone, "Rose, I don't think he belongs here. I think he needs a therapeutic preschool." Rose Messina, the mental health consultant, recognized the stress in the teachers' voices. Their behavior was communicating their feeling of being helpless and that they had run out of ideas and could not think of any solution other than a therapeutic preschool. Recognizing everyone was in high stress and survival mode, Rose understood they needed an emergency plan as the first course of action to help keep everyone feeling safe.

The most pressing need was to create safety and to put together a support plan for Jerome at drop off. This support plan was co-developed with Rose and the teaching team in consultation with his grandmother, Esther. Grandmother was open and receptive as she too observed the intense reaction that Jerome had at drop off. Together they initiated and agreed upon four steps to support Jerome during the morning drop off:

1. Grandma would drop him off 30 minutes before the majority of the children arrived. This would decrease the amount of overstimulation that can occur when all

the children are dropped off at the same time, thus activating his stress response. Reducing the stimulus at drop off can support his regulatory system to maintain the optimal zone of arousal. Grandma worked part-time and had the flexibility to be able to accommodate this earlier drop off.

2. At drop off grandma would sit and read a book to Jerome with his primary teacher, Taz, sitting next to them. The act of reading the book created a calm transition and provided a warm hand off between grandma and his favorite teacher, Taz.

3. A ritual was created at drop off—arrive 30 minutes early, read a book with grandma and teacher Taz, and then there was a special goodbye ritual that had been created between grandma and Jerome. It involved a visual poster on the wall by the door which gave five choices of how you want to say goodbye (handshake, hug, high five, fist bump, or your choice). He usually picked "give a hug."

4. Teacher Taz would hold Jerome's hand and they would walk over to the job board after grandma's departure. Jerome always got first pick of the job he wanted in the classroom that day. This gave him a sense of agency and control and a job that helped him feel a sense of significance and belonging.

While this emergency plan of strategies at drop off was successful in reducing the teacher's stress levels and Jerome's stress reaction, the behavior did continue. There were days when the strategy reduced his reaction, days it did not work, and some days when it seemed to work. More importantly, it provided the needed time and restored energy so that the teaching team could pause, slow down, and think with one another as to what Jerome might be feeling and why he might be entering the classroom in that way (*what is the meaning behind the behavior?*). Teacher Taz was able to quickly volunteer an idea, "Well, *I think he's scared*, but I don't know why he would be scared here."

As the teaching team began to explore, they knew that Jerome's grandma, with all her lived experience, wisdom, and insight, could help them think through the meaning of Jerome's behavior and come up with ideas to help him feel safe. They extended an invitation for tea and to talk more about the morning ritual and how things were going with their new drop-off plan for Jerome. And as the primary teacher and Rose met with grandma, she began to share some of the history: that Jerome had witnessed domestic violence from his father to his mother. Child welfare had been involved. Jerome was placed with grandma and dad had recently been incarcerated. As the conversation progressed between them, they started to wonder what might be happening for Jerome as he enters his classroom and what might help him feel a little bit more in control and safe. And how to acknowledge his fear? Grandma had shared that dad was formerly in the military and he and Jerome used to play with army figures and wear pretend military-style helmets in their play. Grandma said that Jerome loved playing this with his father. The teachers also observed Jerome gravitated to military-style toys. They thought of a new strategy that might help Jerome feel safe.

The teacher had a military-style helmet that she got for her and Jerome. So, they created a narrative that *created agency, voice, and control with his military helmet*. Teacher Taz would greet Jerome at the door, and they continued their new morning drop-off ritual. After grandma left, the teacher would say, "Is it one of the days we need to put on our helmets together and walk around our classroom to make sure everything is safe?" And so, she would get down on his level when he said yes, and most days in the beginning, he said, yes, so they both put their helmets on, and they took a tour together of the entire classroom. Jerome would examine every corner, every nook, and all the toys and say, "This is safe" or "There is no danger here." Jerome never really found an object or part of the room he announced as dangerous. But the act of wearing the powerful helmet (the military helmet giving a sense of power and the relational connection to positive memories of his father) and walking around the room with his teacher (co-regulatory support) gave him a sense of voice, power, and control over his traumatic stress. At first, he did not want his hand to be held, but eventually he could take the teacher's hand and walk around the room.

Change did not come overnight but happened with slow progress. With repetition of the morning rituals that were created at drop off and over time, slowly the shift began where he could enter the classroom with less support. There were more and more days he would walk into the classroom and say to grandma, "You leave. I don't want to read a book. I am going to play with my friends." He came at drop off and ran over to the dramatic play area, no longer showing an interest in this drop-off ritual. On occasion Jerome would have a stressful week due to changes in his visitation with his father and this would trigger a stress reaction. When that happened, Jerome would go back to his military helmet and grab hold of Taz's hand. He learned to find people (his teacher or grandma), objects (his helmet), and activities (the rituals developed at drop off) to help his body feel safe. Jerome had some new resilience practices that helped him cope with his internal stress.

Strategies That Supported Jerome's Ability to Cope and Build Resilience

♦ Recognizing that when Jerome was dysregulated, he had difficulty letting go to play because he was preoccupied with his survival response. *Dysregulated behavior* was the *best way his body knew how to protect himself* from his perceived sense of danger.

♦ Teachers recognized that providing trauma-responsive practices to support Jerome to feel safe helped him spend more time in the zone of optimal arousal, and only then did he start to take an interest in playing with others in the classroom.

♦ Observing the play themes that interest Jerome (military and army play toys) and *using the child's interests to build a trauma-responsive strategy that could help him feel safe* (the helmet reminded him of positive memories of his father).

Trauma-Responsive Practices Used to Support Jerome

◆ *Providing teachers with co-regulatory support and time to talk and reflect.* Recognizing that when teachers are in their survival brain from too much stress, they need co-regulatory support which includes time to talk, reflect, and re-regulate their activated stress response system so that they can begin to access their cortex to problem solve for this child.

◆ *Identifying the sensitive points in the day when Jerome was most dysregulated.* In this case, the teachers identified the transition at drop off as the part of the day when Jerome became most dysregulated.

◆ *Creating emergency trauma-responsive practices to support Jerome to feel safe at drop off.* The plan was co-developed by his teachers, grandma, and the mental health consultant. The emergency individualized support plan included a predictable routine and ritual that would be repeated each day and that felt safe and enjoyable to Jerome, a less abrupt and warmer handout between grandma and the teachers, co-regulatory support from calm and caring adults, a goodbye ritual, and finally offering Jerome some agency, choice, and control by allowing him to choose from the job board.

◆ *Identifying a comfort object* for Jerome that also was connected with positive memories of his father whom he missed. He has positive memories of his father who had previously been in the military, and they used to play with his army toys at home together. By using the military helmets, teachers built on something in play that was of interest to Jerome (army toys) and that conveyed positive relational memories with his dad (army toys and play with his father triggered positive memories relationally in Jerome).

◆ *Repetition of the trauma-responsive practices over time began to create safety.* In other words, using a strategy once will not result in change. The teachers were committed to repeating the strategies so that, over time, Jerome's body could rewire from being on high alert to being more consistently regulated in the zone of optimal arousal.

Reflection/Discussion Questions

◆ Have you observed children in play and found unique play themes that interest them?

◆ Have you ever used that child's play interest/themes in play to support that same child when dysregulated?

CASE STUDY #6: Never Give Up On a Child! There is Always a Way to Help Them Feel Safe

Theresa Sanchez-Perez, Education Manager, Head Start

Theresa Sanchez-Perez, an education manager with 36 years of experience working at an urban Head Start program on the west coast, shared a story of how she and her staff supported a 4-year-old boy named Leonard after he began displaying stress-related behaviors in the classroom. Theresa reveals the struggles and small wins that she and her staff experienced as they worked together to support Leonard and his mother.

A 4-year-old child named Leonard was one of the ten children who returned to our program after we were forced to close our doors for several weeks due to Covid. When Leonard returned, we noticed immediately that he was displaying a lot of stress/trauma-related behaviors.

Leonard was hitting the other children, throwing tables and chairs, and running up to the teachers with objects to hit them; teachers were often covering their faces to protect themselves. During lunch, if we were serving something he didn't like, he would throw the food at the teachers and then yell, "I'm hungry! I want some." Whenever he was playing with his peers, he insisted that everything always had to be his way. He had to be the "winner" and he always wanted to control the rules and the materials during play. Sometimes, Leonard had tantrums where his body was so dysregulated and out of control, we had to move the other nine children from the classroom just to keep them safe. And sadly, we began to notice other children in the classroom were starting to imitate his behavior.

What To Do When Teachers Don't Feel Safe with a Child

When teachers don't feel safe, we should always listen. This means they have run out of ideas, and they are feeling helpless, hopeless, and/or out of control. It is important that teachers have a place to talk, reflect, and share their experiences. This can help support them to immediately feel safe and more regulated and perhaps even increase access to their cortex to think, plan, and examine the next steps.

At the same time, an initial step is to create an emergency plan to help children and teachers feel safe. This emergency plan is a temporary one with concrete agreed-upon strategies to use right away in the classroom to help everyone know what safety steps to take to help everyone feel safe.

A next step would be to develop a longer-term plan to support the child. Multiple observations, strategies that are trauma-responsive, and work for the individual child and that are repeated over time can support their body to feel safe with you and in the classroom.

To this day, we do not know what stressors/trauma Leonard might have experienced because it was never disclosed to us. His family did not want the family service specialist and the mental health consultant to share any specific details with us. We were at a loss as to why he was acting out as he was. But what we did know was that we were now working with a child who was aggressive, not only to children, but also to staff. We felt we tried everything and were stressed and felt a sense of helplessness.

Management arranged to start by having a behavioral specialist come into the classroom and work with us. As a teaching team, we discovered that when Leonard was really distressed, sometimes if we would just hold him and let him cry it out, he would eventually calm. We could see that Leonard wanted to be loved. He wanted to be held, to have some kind of physical touch; through his behavior, he was crying out to us that he did not feel safe and wanted to be cared for.

> The number-one and most powerful pathway to create safety for trauma-impacted children is *relational*. All it takes is one adult to provide an attuned connection with the child to help their survival/hindbrain that is telling them there is danger to feel safe again. We see evidence of this with Leonard. The teachers discovered that if they held him or provided one-to-one connection, it increased his felt sense of safety, prevented triggers, and provided co-regulatory support.

As a staff, we knew that it was important to find opportunities where Leonard could feel a sense of *agency and control* in the classroom. Our first idea was to give him a voice about where he wanted to physically spend time in the classroom. We asked him a simple question: "Leonard, when you arrive each morning, where do you want to sit?" Leonard identified a small table where he could sit by himself. This is where he ate his breakfast, where he completed his activities, where he had his lunch. We could see that "Leonard's table" gave him a sense of control and a feeling of safety by reducing uncertainty (e.g., "This is mine. This is my stuff"). We learned from mom that Leonard liked coloring books and even though we don't typically use them in the classroom, we were flexible as we could see that they could provide an important incentive for Leonard in the classroom. We used and tried a true strategy in early learning classrooms, "*if–then*" to support Leonard throughout the day. "We are going to go to circle first and then you can have the coloring page…First lunch, and then a coloring page…First nap, and then a coloring page."

Another trauma-responsive practice is to provide a child with *agency and control*. Trauma creates for an individual a complete loss of control (unable to fight, flight, freeze, or have any choice or voice during the trauma). The antidote to this loss of control is to provide the child with a sense of agency, choice, voice, and control. It can be in small doses, as the teachers did with Leonard. Asking him, "Where would you like to sit?" is an example of giving agency, choice, and control. This can counteract the internal narrative or feeling of "I am trapped, I have no voice," changing to feeling a sense of power and control.

Leonard also started to vocalize some of his worries—concerns that were likely activating his stress response system and leading to his "fight"-related behaviors. One example we observed was when Leonard started to talk about missing his dad. He would say, "*Quiero mi papá, quiero mi papá.*" Of course, we shared this with Leonard's mom. She told us that Leonard's father was out of the country and there was no way that Leonard could speak with him. We wanted to be respectful of this family's privacy while also feeling some responsibility to be an advocate for Leonard—to amplify his voice and what we were learning about the feelings and needs he was trying to communicate to his caregivers. We told her that perhaps Leonard did not understand *why* he couldn't talk with his dad or see his dad, and this was probably a big reason why he was struggling so much, so we asked her to share a picture of Leonard's dad. Mom was initially resistant to these ideas. But then one day a few weeks later, I opened my computer and saw an email from Leonard's mom. And low and behold, my heart was beating so fast, there was a picture of Leonard's dad! The timing was really something. This was a morning when Leonard was having one of the worst outbursts that he had ever had. As soon as I saw the photo, I walked over to Leonard and said, "Leonard, look who is on my computer." And I turned it around, and it was his dad. When Leonard discovered the photo was his dad, the look on his face was so touching. He started crying, "My *papi*, my *papi*, my *papi!*" I printed out the picture and laminated it. Leonard held on to that photo all day long. I noticed that whenever he was really frustrated, he would hold it even tighter.

Do I Need to Know the Trauma History to Help a Child?

You do not need to know the history to help a child. All trauma-responsive strategies are designed to help a child feel safe. People, places, objects, and activities are all pathways that could potentially help a child feel safe. For Leonard it was a teacher, close proximity to an adult, a photo image of his father and giving him agency, choice, and control in situations. It was never giving up; it was being a careful observer of what triggers him and what helps him feel safe.

Months Later and Leonard is Now in Kindergarten

I happened to run into Leonard and his mom a few months after he started kindergarten. I went to say hello to them, and mom started crying at that point. She apologized for not being more open about what Leonard was going through and what she had been going through the previous year.

We can never know why a family does not accept services. Fear of deportation? Lack of trust in systems? In a current state of trauma and unable to feel safe enough to trust or think or even reason clearly? Because relational trust has not been built with the teachers? These are just a few of many possibilities. Can the child be helped if the family does not accept services? This is one of the biggest questions an early childhood educator has. It is common for early childhood educators to say, "I cannot help the child unless the family changes or gets help." The research shows that children are building one million new neurosynaptic connectors every second and all it takes is one adult in their life to build trust and safety and to support healing from toxic situations. Teachers can make a difference every day, even when that child returns home to situations that are stressful.

Good news! As you will see from research, practicing trauma-responsive strategies rewires the brain—and used along with other strategies (e.g., nurturing and responsive relationships/safe predictable environments), we can help children repair some of the damaging and long-term adverse impacts of trauma.

(Harvard's Center on the Developing Child, 2022)

Strategies That Supported Leonard's Ability to Cope and Build Resilience

♦ The adults did not feel safe and were highly stressed. When this happens, adults will be operating in their "survival" brain and will be more reactive, stopping at the voice, "What is wrong with you?" with the trajectory of reactions being to blame, shame, criticize, punish, or even expel the child to make the bad behavior stop. In this story, the adults' stress was recognized and listening was priotizied. It was important to listen to how the teachers felt, and what they were experiencing and needed.

♦ After listening to the teachers and supporting them to regulate, the teachers might have had more access to that next voice, "What is your behavior communicating?" With this voice, the cortex is open and they are more likely able to reason, problem solve, and slow down to think of what will help Leonard feel safe.

♦ Creating an emergency plan so that teachers and children feel safe was a priority for everyone. Feeling safe is critical to be able to be present for all the children in the classroom.

♦ Creating a long-term plan with trauma-responsive strategies helped Leonard feel safe. After careful observation, the staff came up with some hypotheses as to what his behavior was communicating. The teachers wanted to help him feel safe, provide him with connection, and give him a felt sense of agency and control.

Trauma-Responsive Practices Used to Support Leonard

◆ *Provide him with positive, attuned relational connection with teachers and his father* (papi). The teachers recognized that Leonard needed positive relational connection. When he was in distress they held him, hugged him, and let him cry without trying to correct, direct, or move him to a better solution. They found this comforted him more readily and was just what he needed to feel safe. They also found that the photo of his *papi* helped him. This visual made him feel connected to his father in the way he needed throughout the day.

◆ *Offer opportunities for agency and control.* When Leonard was offered simple choices of how to play with materials, or when he had control over what "stuff" was his and that he did not have to share, this gave him a perceived sense of agency and control in his environment.

◆ *If–then schedules.* The use of a visual aid such as an if–then schedule can help trauma-impacted children whose bodies feel overwhelmed by so much stimulus or too many choices to feel safe. Why? Because when Leonard felt overwhelmed by too many choices or his cortex could not focus or listen, the visual helped make his world less overwhelming and more manageable. He now only has two simple choices: *if* (you wash your hands) *then* (you can do that thing you love, like go outside to play). Some programs call it a first–then schedule. This can help reduce the volume of overwhelm the child is experiencing in the moment.

Reflection/Discussion Questions

◆ Have you ever not known the history of the child but still been able to help them?

♦ Were you able to find a pathway that helped the child feel safe and regulated? Was it a person? a place? an object? Or was it an activity that helped the child feel safe and calm?

♦ Do you have an experience helping a child, even when the family was not accepting of support services or not willing to collaborate in conversation about their child?

References

Harvard's Center on the Developing Child (2022). *Brain architecture.* Retrieved from https://developingchild.harvard.edu/science/key-concepts/brain-architecture/

Perry, B. (2014). *Rhythm regulates the brain.* Retrieved from https://attachmentdisorderhealing.com/developmental-trauma-3/

Conclusion

It is the fundamental right of all children to have joy in their early learning experiences. Play and joy can come in simple moments throughout the day if we intentionally plan for play-powered environments. The result of these small doses of present-moment joy, even for just a few seconds or a minute, can release positive chemicals that impact and improve children's mental and physical health and overall wellness, and prevent long-term adverse outcomes of stress and trauma.

We close with the wise words of two early childhood professionals. Valentina Torres, mental health specialist, reinforces that our work—serving young children and families impacted by stress and trauma—is *hard*. She encourages us to collaborate and build partnerships to share the responsibilities and joys of the important work we do. She also reminds us that growth comes from taking risks that allow us to learn and grow:

> It can be really hard when children are engaging in difficult behaviors. Being gentle with oneself, acknowledging where you really are at, is going to be really important. If you've got the chance to partner with a mental health consultant and you can be honest about what you don't know, what you're afraid of, you can really grow from that.

DOI: 10.4324/9781003326113-7

Barb O'Neil, founder of Transform Challenging Behavior, reminds us that early educators hold a tremendous amount of practice wisdom about the value of play and playful learning in young children's lives. She urges all of us to trust our professional knowledge and remain strong advocates for young children's right to play even when we face resistance:

> A lot of our early childhood teachers intuitively understand the power of play for learning and healing. Seeing these stories and strategies and collective knowledge in this book, I hope that it helps them to trust what they know in their heart. To see themselves as advocates for what children really need, whether that's making a small change in their classroom, talking to a parent, or if they're in an environment that doesn't support play, maybe talking to their administrator or closing the door at times and letting play go just a little longer. The most important thing is that early educators really feel a sense that they are not alone. When you feel that advocating for play is difficult work, remember that you have a community. We're all out here doing this work in different ways. We can be fortified by knowing that we are all working with a shared goal: *we are supporting children to learn and thrive through the power of play.*

Bessel van der Kolk (2014) reminds us that individual and collective healing is supported when "we feel safely held in the hearts and minds of the people who love us" (p. 350). We encourage readers to join us in focusing our love and commitment for children by safely holding their right to play—to support their development, learning, stress reduction, and healing—in our hearts and minds.

Reference

van der Kolk, B. A. (2014). *The body keeps the score: Brain, mind and body in the healing of trauma.* New York, NY: Penguin Books.

Resources

Books for Adults

Parenting

♦ *Parenting from the Inside Out* by Daniel J. Siegel and Mary Hartzell.

In *Parenting from the Inside Out*, child psychiatrist Daniel J. Siegel, M.D., and early childhood expert Mary Hartzell, M.Ed., explore the extent to which our childhood experiences shape the way we parent.

♦ *The Whole Brain Child* by Daniel J. Siegel and Tina Payne Bryson.

In this pioneering, practical book, Daniel J. Siegel, neuro-psychiatrist and parenting expert Tina Payne Bryson offer a revolutionary approach to child rearing with 12 key strategies that foster healthy brain development, leading to calmer, happier children.

♦ *Out of Sync Child: Recognizing and Coping with Sensory Processing Disorder* and *The Out-of-Sync Child Has Fun: Activities for Kids with Sensory Processing Disorder* by Carol Stock Kranowitz.

This book presents more than 100 playful activities specially designed for kids with sensory processing disorder. Each activity in this inspiring and practical book is SAFE—sensorimotor, appropriate, fun, and easy—to help develop and organize a child's brain and body.

Adults Impacted by Trauma

♦ *The Body Keeps the Score: Brain, Mind, and Body in the Healing of Trauma* by Bessel van der Kolk.

This book uses recent scientific advances to show how trauma literally reshapes both body and brain, compromising sufferers' capacities for pleasure, engagement, self-control, and trust. The author explores innovative treatments—from neurofeedback and meditation to sports, drama, and yoga—that offer new paths to recovery by activating the brain's natural neuroplasticity.

Books for Children

Promoting Sensory-Emotional Literacy and Body Awareness and Managing Big Emotions

♦ *Listening to My Body* by Gabi Garcia
  An engaging and interactive book that guides children through the practice of naming their feelings and the physical sensations that accompany them. (Available in Spanish as *Escuchando a Mi Cuerpo*.)

♦ *Calm-Down Time* by Elizabeth Verdick
  This book offers toddlers simple tools to release strong feelings, express them, and calm themselves down.

♦ *Understanding My Brain: Becoming Human(E)!* by Julie Kurtz (ages 4–8 or 5–10)
  When children learn about how their brain works, it enables better decision making and choices to help them feel safe, find calm, and build social-emotional skills. Think of this as a science book for children ages 4–8 and 5–10, made fun through the lens of four animals. Lizzie the Lizard Plays the Hindbrain, Malcolm the Meerkat Plays the Amygdala, Elsie the Elephant Plays the Limbic Brain, and Ozzie the Owl Plays the Prefrontal Cortex and teaches children to build a toolkit to help their bodies feel safe and calm.

♦ *Breathe Like a Bear* by Kira Willey
  Thirty mindful moments for kids to feel calm.

♦ *Mindful Kids: 50 Mindfulness Activities Cards (Ages 4–99)* by Whitney Steward and Mina Braun
  This boxed card deck includes 50 creative mindfulness games, visualizations, and exercises divided into five categories to help children feel grounded, find calm, improve focus, practice loving kindness, and relax.

♦ *Yoga Pretzels: 50 Fun Yoga Activities for Kids and Grownups* by Tara Guber
Practice bending, twisting, breathing, relaxing, and more with *Yoga Pretzels*, a vibrant and colorful set of illustrated cards that provide a healthy dose of fun and education to promote regulation.

♦ *Mind Bubbles* by Heather Krantz
Mind Bubbles presents an easy way for young children to work with their breath while noting thoughts and feelings passing and popping like bubbles. The book is a clear, concise, and secular explanation of mindfulness that children ages 4–8 will understand and want to try for themselves.

♦ *Mindful Moves* by Nicole Cardoza
Mindful Moves introduces kids to simple mindfulness activities that are fun, easy to remember, and available for kids to turn to any time the need arises, no matter where they are.

♦ *B is for Breathe* by Melissa Munro Boyd
From the letter A to the letter Z, *B is for Breathe* celebrates the many ways children can express their feelings and develop coping skills at an early age.

Books for Children who Have Been Through Scary Things

♦ *Once I was Very Very Scared* by Chondra Ghosh Ippen
https://piploproductions.com/stories/once/ (free downloadable versions in many languages)
This story was written to help children and grown-ups understand how stress can affect children and provide ways to help them.

Death or Loss

♦ *When Dinosaurs Die* by Laurie Krasny Brown and Marc Brown
Straightforward and comprehensive, this indispensable book is a comforting aid to help young kids and families through a difficult time in their lives. No one can really

understand death, but to children, the passing away of a loved one can be especially perplexing and troublesome.

Scared at Night of Monsters

◆ *Go Away, Big Green Monster!* by Ed Emberley
This book helps children to overcome bedtime frights. As kids turn the die-cut pages of this vibrantly illustrated book, they'll watch the Big Green Monster grow before their very eyes. Then, when they're ready to show him who's in charge, they'll turn the remaining pages and watch him disappear!

Divorce or Parent Separation

◆ *It's Not Your Fault, Koko Bear* by Vicki Lansky
The story of a lovable bear who doesn't want to have two homes, this book reassures children that their feelings are natural, their parents will still love and care for them, and the divorce is not their fault.

◆ *The Invisible String* and *The Invisible Leash* by Patrice Karst
The Invisible String addresses feelings of separation anxiety, something that many children experience in the midst of a transition that impacts their time with loved ones. In the story, a mother describes to her children that they are all connected by "An Invisible String made of love." *The Invisible Leash* is about losing a pet.

◆ *You Weren't with Me* by Chandra Ghosh Ippen
(Available in English and Spanish)
This story was designed to help parents and children talk about difficult separations, reconnect, and find their way back to each other.

Moving or Saying Goodbye

◆ *Moving to the Neighborhood (Daniel Tiger's Neighborhood)* by Jason Fruchter
In this sweet board book, Daniel Tiger gets a new neighbor. Moving is scary at first, but the new neighbor soon feels right at home.

Apps

♦ *Trigger Stop: Sensory and Emotional Check-In Ages 3–8* by Julie Kurtz at Center *for Optimal Brain Integration*
www.optimalbrainintegration.com/app-1
A free 22-minute video and free downloadable version of the app and a user guide in English and Spanish are available.

♦ *Trigger Stop: Sensory and Emotional Check-In*
Application designed for children developmentally aged 3–8 years. This smartphone/tablet app is intended for use for children who might not be able to access their words when their emotions are intense, and they become dysregulated in the moment. Whether a result of a trauma trigger or emotional trigger in that moment, a child may not have access to the executive parts of their brain in charge of reasoning, logic, or words.

Website

♦ *Transform Challenging Behavior*
Transform Challenging Behavior (TCB) was formed by Barb O'Neill, Ed.D., in 2016 based on a desire to get teachers simple but powerful strategies they could use to prevent challenging behavior and support the children who exhibit it. TCB offers an array of online learning opportunities, including: free live events; downloadable resources; the annual TCB Online Conference; and the TCB Teachers' Club, an online professional development membership. Each week, Barb's challenging behavior tips are delivered to over 100,000 educators via her weekly email. transformchallengingbehavior.com.

A Note on the Cover

Isaac's Mural

We chose this cover because we were moved by the story of a kindergarten teacher in California who brings trauma-responsive practices and the power of play to support children impacted by toxic stress. This mural was created by a young boy named Isaac who, while attending Mr. Kurada's kindergarten class, was experiencing cumulative risk factors and traumatic stress.

Teacher Ryan Kurada and his class were working on an imaginary city improvement project where the children were asked to make plans for improving many different areas of the city where the school was located. As a class, they were imagining a model city that would be a better and more interesting place for kids to live in. Mr. Kurada asked: "Isaac, what do you want to do to improve the arts in our community?" He responded,

> Mr. Kurada, I have an idea to improve our community with a painting. I want this city to have more art everywhere. There is a blank wall on a building by my house and it's kind of boring. My plan is to add a painting that shows all the people in the city working together.

Mr. Kurada brought some canvas in the following week and Isaac's idea turned into a giant 30-foot mural that all the students in the classroom worked on collectively to paint. When Isaac's mother got to see the mural her son made, she cried tears of joy. Mr. Kurada says, "It's so important to *follow the child's strengths, their passions, and their interests. It could change a life."*

Mr. Kurada exemplifies trauma-responsive practices by carefully observing his students and their interests and developmental needs and alters his behavior as he thinks to himself, "What is the best way to build a relationship with this child?," "What are this student's passions and strengths and how can I build on and harness them?," and "How can I point out a child's strengths so both the child and the child's family can see them too?"

Teacher Ryan Kurada's story is the central thread for all our books—that it only takes one adult in the life of a child to provide the relational connection and attunement that will buffer their stress, uncover their hidden strengths, and build their resilience.

Isaac, now a sixth-grader, and Teacher Ryan.
Source: Ryan Kurada.

Isaac and his mother.
Source: Ryan Kurada.